Also by **Diwan Jarmani Dass**

- Maharaja

Maharani

**A fabulous collection of adventures
of
Indian Princesses and Royal Mistresses**

Diwan Jarmani Dass
Rakesh Bhan Dass

HIND POCKET BOOKS

Note:

While every care has been taken to ascertain the accuracy of facts and pictures, any mistake is neither intended nor deliberate. The book is based on historical facts as recorded by the author who was a Diwan in many royal states of India.

MAHARANI
Copyright © Rakesh Dass, 2007
All rights reserved.

This Edition, 2008
First Reprint: 2009
Second Reprint: 2011

ISBN 978-81-216-1208-1

Published by
HIND POCKET BOOKS PVT. LTD.
J-40, Jorbagh Lane, New Delhi-110003
Tel: +011 24620063, 24621011 • Fax: 24645795
Email: contact@fullcirclebooks.in • *website:* www.fullcirclebooks.in

Designing & Typesetting: *SCANSET*

J-40, Jorbagh Lane, New Delhi-110003

Printed at Yash Printographers, B-123, Sector-10, Noida-201301

PRINTED IN INDIA

08/11/03/07/20/SCANSET/DE/YP/YP/OP195/NP195

Contents

❀ *Rare Photographs* ❀

1

Why Women?

I was only thirty when His Highness the Aga Khan said to me: "Jarmani (as he used to call me in a familiar way), if you are successful with women, you are successful in life."

I was then his guest at the Savoy Hotel, London, and attending a dinner party to which he had invited Mr. Edwin Montague, the then Secretary of State, and many other prominent personalities. I had just danced a tango with Princess Andree Carron Aga Khan, his French consort and one of the most beautiful and cultured women of her time, when I received this advice by the Aga Khan.

The advice, though given in a jocular manner and in a jolly mood, went home, and ever afterwards I made efforts to become more friendly with Maharanis, Princesses and other women in all walks of life rather than with men. My friendship with them paid me good dividends besides giving me mental happiness. All my life, I was helped and favoured by Maharanis, Princesses and society women not only in India but throughout the world. I became intimate with women of several nationalities in different parts of the world.

Wherever I went I always made it a point to cultivate the friendship of women. However, I always remembered what a French author had said and also what the irate Prophet Mohammed said about the caprice of women and their idiosyncrasies. This is also vividly depicted by Hercodpules in his book about King Candleus who had a beautiful Queen and was sorry that no one except himself admired her beauty. He wished to be envied for having such beautiful wife. Unknown to the Queen, he hid his Prime Minister Dyges behind a curtain so that he might have a good look at the Queen when she was taking a bath. The Queen however saw the feet of the Prime Minister sticking out and took immediate offence. She caught him and warned him that he must either die for this or kill the King and marry her. Dyges was very happy to make the choice. He killed the King and founded his own dynasty.

It is a universal truth that tender feelings forge the bonds of attraction between the sexes. This attraction is commonly spoken of as love and the sentiment is identified with the sexual impulse. Sexual attraction throughout the animal kingdom and even in the vegetable kingdom is loosely spoken of as a manifestation of love and hence should be regarded as an almost primordial quality of protoplasm. We quote Schiller: "Man is ruled by hunger and love. Nature has her hymn of love. Just as man and woman attract one another, oxygen attracts hydrogen and in loving union with it forms water. Potassium phosphate entertains such violent longings for oxygen that even under water they burn and thus unite themselves with the beloved object. It is love in the form of magnetic attraction which links stone to stone, earth to earth, stars to stars and gravitation holds together the mighty edifice of the globe on which we stand, and its name in human terms is love."

In Paris where I spent the greater part of my youth and

middle age visiting Maharanis and Princesses every evening, I had 20 to 25 women, including foreign women of aristocracy, to choose from. But I did not confine myself to high society alone. I was equally keen to meet girls selling flowers in the streets, and shop-girls.

I had great opportunities to be able to entertain women because of the large amount of money at my disposal from the Privy Purses of the Rulers whom I accompanied. Therefore, **what I write in this book is from my personal experience of women of yesterday and today.**

Since I first went to France for my education several decades ago, during the First World War, there has been a revolution in the minds of men and women, not only in India but throughout the world. The mental outlook of women, their dress, their behaviour towards men, their sex appetites and their sense of loyalty towards their husbands and even lovers, have undergone a sea change. In this book you will see how, slowly but surely, this transformation has come about.

Likewise, in the chapters which follow, I shall depict how it was the influence of the British residing in India and the deliberate policy of the British Government in the 20th century that brought about a complete change in the character of Maharanis, Princesses, and women in the high strata of society. The so-called emancipation of women and the so-called modem education imparted to the women in India, offering them high positions, not only in the Government but also in commerce and industry, in the Army, Navy, Air Force and other departments of administration, engendered a mental climate which adversely governed their social ways.

Later, I shall deal with the behaviour of women in India and abroad today in sex and other matters. But before I talk of social laws, divorce, separation, inheritance etc. in European countries, I shall devote myself to the status of women as it stands today in our society.

The homes which were like paradise before the so-called emancipation of women have become, in most cases, a blazing till due to the disparity in thought and culture between husband and wife, between father and daughter. The result is that 55 out of every 100 homes in India, in the higher strata of society and even in the upper middle classes, get disrupted. I have talked to many of my friends in this high society about this. Most of them admit that due to preoccupation with politics, social life and travels abroad, their wives have completely lost touch with their husbands, homes and children.

In the family of prehistoric times and even in the primitive days, the woman was shared by the husband and his brothers. But today the wife is shared by his intimate friends. It is a pitiable sight to see that most of the women employed in the Government departments and business and industrial houses have to surrender to the outrageous demands of their superior officers. Recently, a sensational report was submitted by Mr. M. M. Basu, Chief Secretary of the West Bengal Government. Mr. Raghunath Banerjee, Joint Secretary and Commissioner of the Presidency Division and Special Officer of Indo-Pak boundary in Bengal, had in a short period illegitimate and immoral connections with 50 women whom he enticed to his bed by offers of employment, increment and promotion. He was prematurely retired for indulging in sex orgies in his air-conditioned office room furnished with a sofa set and a dressing table at the state expense. If one Joint Secretary can entice 50 married and unmarried women to his bed, how many women secretaries and other officials in the Governments of the States, numbering thousands, must be doing so following the pattern of licentious living.

It is the economy of the country and the environment in which we live today and the indiscriminate appointment of women in Administrative Departments that have brought about these catastrophic changes in the morals of the people. I hold that women can be useful not only looking after their homes and children but also doing social work, which is compatible with their physical strength and talent, working in hospitals, in nursing homes, in vegetable and food development enterprises, in milk schemes, and in social reforms and various other departments. Happiness in the family can be assured only if there are two spheres, one to be controlled by men and the other by women. How happy a home can be if women make that home comfortable, beautiful and hospitable and look after the development of their children who are our future citizens. Formerly, men worked in the fields, fought in wars and undertook hazardous jobs and performed their duties more efficiently than today. These days men go back home only to find their wives away or busy in offices and in some cases, on official tours in India and abroad. Finding themselves in utter loneliness they then try to find solace in the company of other women. This disrupts society on the whole and at the base, and unless social changes are brought about in a revolutionary way, there can be no peace and happiness in the family. The same maxim applies to homes in other countries of the world. In my opinion, women's main job is to look after husbands and children and the formation of their character.

The efficiency of husbands and the well-being of children depend on the comfort and care they get at home. What a beautiful home it is where the wife is devoted to her husband and children!

2

Cherchez la Femme

'Cherchez la femme' is a French saying which means that in all affairs and activities of man — intrigues, business, wars, love affairs, civil and military administration, politics — and his predicaments and catastrophes, there is always a woman at the bottom. And so it has been at all times and in all societies.

I first came into contact with Maharajas and Maharanis when I was invited by His Highness Maharaja Jagatjit Singh, Ruler of Kapurthala State — an important Sikh State in the Punjab — to spend a few days in summer with him at his Chateau de Kapurthala at Mussoorie — a hill-station in Uttar Pradesh. This chateau is a very fine piece of architecture with beautiful turrets in the style of the French chateaus owned by the aristocracy of France — Princes, Dukes, Counts and Barons. It is situated at an altitude of 7,500 feet with a spacious tennis court, flower gardens and rare plants overlooking the Himalayan peaks clad in snow which shines dazzlingly on a sunny day. The Maharaja was fascinated by my tennis, as I had won the Singles' Championship of the University of Punjab, beating the best tennis player of the Government College, Lahore, by the name of Mr. Sunder Das who afterwards became the Cambridge Blue in Tennis and was known as the best tennis player in the University of Punjab at that time. The Maharaja was so pleased with my victory in winning the championship that in an open Investiture Reception (Durbar) he pinned on my chest with his own hands a gold medal with the inscription "Champion of the Punjab University, offered by His Highness Maharaja Jagatjit Singh of Kapurthala."

My father, grandfather, great-grandfather and even earlier ancestors were Ministers and Diwans of the Indian States and, in accordance with the traditions of the States, the sons of the Diwans were given high positions from an early age. So, besides my academic qualifications and the University Championship in Tennis Singles, I had the privilege of being introduced to the Court of Kapurthala as the scion of the family which had rendered great services to the Maharaja and his ancestors.

When there was a dispute regarding the will of Maharaja Nihal Singh, father of Maharaja Randhir Singh, my grandfather Diwan Mathura Dass, was sent to London to plead the case with the Secretary of State for India, as the Maharaja had lost the appeal before the Viceroy. The Secretary of State for India, with the approval of Her Imperial Majesty Queen Victoria of England and Empress of India, got the decision of the Viceroy reversed and the will made by Maharaja Nihal Singh was declared null and void. This will, if upheld, would have divided the State into three equal parts among his three sons. It was made by Maharaja Nihal Singh only to please his favourite Maharani who had two sons by him. His eldest son, Maharaja Randhir Singh, born to the senior Maharani, who was no longer in favour with him, was to succeed his father as his sole heir to the throne. By this will, made by his father, he was to be deprived of succession. The case was therefore fought judicially in London in the Court of the Secretary of State for India. Queen Victoria, after the Revolution of 1857, had pledged to the Rulers of the States to safeguard their dignity, honour and privileges and to uphold the prevailing laws of succession.

The Secretary of State for India gave his decision that Maharaja Randhir Singh should rule over the entire State of Kapurthala while his half-brothers were to be given handsome annual cash allowances, but asked to live outside the State so that no cause for conflict between them should occur. They lived 15 miles away from Kapurthala in a town called Jullundur. Maharaja Randhir Singh, grandfather of Jagatjit Singh, was extremely pleased with the services rendered by my grandfather in London in getting the decision of the Viceroy of India reversed, and as a reward, gave him thousands of acres of land, precious jewels and a large amount of money. I may also mention that my great-grandfather, Diwan Ramjas, was Regent of the State during the minority of Maharaja Jagatjit Singh, and ruled the State on his behalf for 13 years as Jagatjit Singh was only five years old when his father Maharaja Kharak Singh died. My father, Diwan Daulat Ram, a Minister of the Government of Kapurthala, was a favourite of the Maharaja and travelled with him on his tours to Europe. With this background of family history and personal qualifications, the Maharaja always treated me, even during my college days, with paternal care.

The Maharaja played good tennis but was often in the habit of bending too low while returning a low ball. He expressed his desire to have me in Mussoorie for the summer vacation to play tennis with him and act as his Aide-de-Camp. The Chateau de Kapurthala was the venue for the cream of society in Mussoorie during the summer season where fancy dress balls, dinners, suppers and garden parties were held three to four times a week and to which hundreds of British officers,

English ladies and Indians of high society, including Maharajas and Maharanis, were invited.

On the first day of my arrival at Mussoorie, I was put up in 'Sunny View' — a luxurious State guest-house — and was invited to dinner by the Maharaja. At the dinner there were only six persons: the Maharaja, his Spanish Maharani named Prem Kaur whom the Maharaja married according to Sikh rites, his lady companion Mlle. Louise Dujon who later married to Mr. E. M. Atkinson (a Tutor in Chiefs College, Lahore), two senior household officers and myself. When drinks were being served, I was asked what I would like to drink. I replied that I would like to take lemonade. At my request, the Maharani, who seemed to have a soft corner for me, asked Slawick, the Maitre d' Hotel, to bring French lemonade for me. I had three glasses in all. Only later was I told that it actually was French champagne. This is how I was introduced to champagne and to the European way of life. During that period, the British had become very friendly with the Maharajas and their staff-officers. Due to the fact that the political movement led by the Indian National Congress was taking firm root, the Viceroy and the British Civil Service made every effort to check this movement by wooing the Maharajas and their Ministers, and showing them extra favours and personal friendship which were not their destiny before that period. The British Officers and their women mixed with the Maharajas and their staff on intimate terms and went to the extent of having love affairs with them.

3

The Himalayan Home of Gaiety

The Maharaja of Kapurthala and the Maharajas of other States like Patiala, Rampur, Rajpipla, Panna, Baroda, Nabha and Jind, gave sumptuous dinner parties at Mussoorie to which they invited the cream of the society of Mussoorie as well as British officers and civilians, both English and Indian, along with their consorts.

I well remember the several dinner parties and receptions held at Chateau de Kapurthala during the period of my stay there. Balls were very popular, particularly fancy dress balls where men and women disguised themselves in various types of dresses, a lot of alcoholic drinks and sumptuous food were served and merrymaking went on throughout the night. Men and women — both Indian and English — quickly got intoxicated. Printed Dance Cards were issued to the participants before the ball to make reservations for dancing, and it was very seldom that British women refused the invitation of an Indian to dance and to reserve dances for him in their dance cards. While dancing was going on, dozens of couples would disappear into the park and miss their dancing reservations. What happened in the park is left to readers to guess, but my Indian friends told me that they had tremendous success with English women. There were benches in the dark, secluded places in the park where the couples enjoyed each other's company to their heart's content. After the ball, the Maharajas, Maharanis, Princesses, society ladies, high British Military Officers, civilians, Indians holding high positions in the Government, and their consorts and relatives, had to ride in rickshaws pulled by porters in magnificent uniforms. It was at that time that pairing was secretly decided and the couples got into these rickshaws and went around Camel's Back, a circular road behind the hill facing the beautiful scenery of the high mountains, snow and perpetual greenery. Here the couples spent hours before the women were dropped at their residences. Some bold women did not hesitate to take their lovers to their houses to share their beds. Dances, skating and carnivals were held in which couples took part and won prizes.

I must tell the reader that, from the beginning of the first World War in 1914 up to its end in 1945, Mussoorie, Simla, Dalhousie, Nainital, Darjeeling, Mount Abu, Ootacamund and other hill-stations had become the summer resorts of the British Officers and their families as well as of the ruling Indian Princes and their families, along with the aristocracy and elite of the Indian society. As the Senior Military Officers could not go to the hills for the whole summer, their womenfolk went there for the whole season and normally senior Military Officers, Generals and Colonels asked their Aides-de-Camp, Captains or Majors to look after their wives, turn by turn, when they got leave to spend a few weeks in these resorts. Naturally, the young military officers in hilarious mood indulged in such acts with the young wives of the senior officers which they would have probably refrained from in the plains. The whole atmosphere of these summer resorts was nothing but gaiety, frivolity and sex indulgence.

There was yet another stratagem used to capture the hearts of British women. They loved riding horses and as hired horses in these health resorts were of very poor breed and physique, British and Indian women could not have a pleasure ride on them. Of course, they were used for hiking and going on the top of the hills, but British women who loved riding on horses preferred to have good horses which were not available except in the stables of the Maharajas.

I remember how Maharaja Jagatjit Singh felt fascinated by a beautiful English woman and invited her many times for dinners and balls. She accepted his invitations gladly, but when it came to flirtation, or dining or supping with the Maharaja alone, she made one excuse or the other and the Maharaja was disappointed. One evening, he told her that he would send her two horses for riding and that she could go for riding excursions with her boyfriend. She was indeed very pleased to go for a ride. After a few days when she and her boyfriend got used to riding these beautiful horses, the Maharaja asked me not to send the horses any more. She came begging for the loan of the horses and in return agreed to consider any proposal which the Maharaja would make to her. The Maharaja asked her to have supper with him alone in his chateau and she accepted the invitation. The Maharaja spent a glorious night with her. After some time, the Maharaja gave her a pair of his best riding horses as a gift, besides jewellery. Later she became his regular mistress for many summers.

Other contacts which I had with women were in Paris. I was attending lectures on political economy at the Sorbonne University after learning French. During my first visit to Paris I stayed as a paying guest in the house of a very respectable Parisian, Madame Dujon, the mother of Mlle. Louise Dujon whom I have mentioned earlier. The family consisted of Madame

Dujon, her grown-up daughter Lily who was in my age-group, and her brother Pierre. As they did not know a word of English or any other language which I knew, I picked up French within six months and began to follow lectures in political economy. I was treated like a member of the family and given excellent food.

When I returned to India in 1917, Maharaja Jagatjit Singh of Kapurthala felt happy that I could speak French fluently and appointed me Deputy Director of Education on which post I remained for two years. Then I rose to the position of Military Secretary at the age of 27, and after two years I was appointed a Minister.

4

In the Hall of Mirrors

Maharaja Jagatjit Singh of Kapurthala was invited by the British
Government to Versailles for the signing of the Peace Treaty
between the Germans and the Allied Nations, along with Maharaja
Ganga Singh of Bikaner who was a member of the Supreme War
Council. I was on the staff of the Maharaja and had the honour
and privilege of witnessing the grand ceremony of the signing
of the Treaty on the afternoon of the 28th of June 1919. The
ceremony was an impressive spectacle. In the gallery of glasses
and at a horse-shoe table in the middle, hedged by large mirrors
on one side and by rows and rows of tabourets under a scroll
proclaiming *"Le Roi Gouverne, Par Lui-Meme"* sat the Tiger of
France, Clemenceau, with his short legs just touching the floor.
He had remembered the birth of the Hohenzollern Empire and
here and now he wanted to witness its death. Wilson and Lloyd
George, President of USA and Prime Minister of Great Britain,
respectively, took their seats on the right and left of George
Clemenceau, the hero of France.

Before I proceed further, it may be of interest to know
about the gallery of glasses where this Treaty was signed. The

gallery of glasses was used daily by the king as a passage and on special occasions to receive ambassadors of foreign countries. It is 73 meters in length, 10.50 meters in width, and 12.30 meters in height, and became of historical significance because of many events such as of the presentation of the Ambassador of Siam in 1686 and Ambassador of Persia (Iran) in 1750, the marriage of Duke of Bourgoyne with Marie Adelaide de Savoie in 1897, the fancy masked ball on the occasion of the marriage of Marie Antoinette with Dauphin in 1770, the proclamation of the Emperor of Germany in 1871 and finally, the signature of the Treaty of Versailles.

It is an amusing historical fact that when the Ambassador of Siam presented his credentials to the King in the gallery of glasses in 1636, he had to crawl on his belly for 73 meters, and after the presentation of the credentials, had to crawl back in the same fashion, keeping his face towards the king and not his back as a mark of respect for the king. The Ambassador must have been an athlete and a strong man. It was a manifestation of the staunch loyalty of the King of Siam to the King of France.

On the history-making day on which the Treaty of Versailles was signed in 1919, the air was bright and the atmosphere festive. Clemenceau said in a solemn tone. "Let the Germans come." The Germans entered escorted by ushers. Nobody rose to greet them. The Germans were the first to sign and they were followed by Wilson with the delegates. In less than an hour, all the signatures were affixed.

Outside, guns boomed, aeroplanes dipped low and the fountains spurt out for the first time. The big three, Clemenceau, Wilson and Lloyd George, walked together and the multitude outside shouted "*Vive* Clemenceau, *Vive* Wilson, *Vive* Lloyd George."

The same night, at Palace de L'Opera, such unparalleled scenes of enthusiasm and outburst of joy and gratitude were manifested by a million people as I have never witnessed throughout my life. When Clemenceau appeared on the balcony of the Opera, the whole of Paris applauded.

The members of the German Delegation were lodged in a house at a short distance from Chateau de Versailles, and the entrances to this house were barricaded and guarded by French troops. It was on this unforgettable and historic occasion that I had the opportunity to see the great men of that time. Maharaja Jagatjit Singh of Kapurthala and I went to see Woodrow Wilson at the mansion at 13 Place des Etats-Unis. He was wearing a black coat and striped trousers and a high-collar cravat with pince-nez. We talked for about ten minutes. He was accompanied by his second wife Edith Gait whom he had married after the death of his first wife. He talked of humanity and said that national interest should be expendable for the good of all humanity.

Wilson looked serene, pensive and philosophical during our ten-minute talk with him. He stood for the whole human race with compassion for all people and condemnation for none. All the time he championed the cause of the League of Nations. Clemenceau and the delegation from the Germans laughed and sneered at the proposed League of Nations. Wilson's faith in the goodness of God and the essential nobility of man weathered all the vicissitudes of his life.

I also met Lloyd George in London at a garden party at the Buckingham Palace and had a short talk with him. He was very authoritative and frowned at anyone who came in his way while he was walking. I got to know Clemenceau intimately when he came to Kapurthala as the guest of the Maharaja of Kapurthala and stayed at the Palace. He was in the habit of saying *"Je m'en fou"* (I don't care) if he did not agree with any of our suggestions. He made a brilliant speech at the banquet when he compared Kapurthala to Athens, the cradle of civilisation of the East, and when I asked him whether we could publish his speech in the newspapers, he said, *"Je m'en fou"*.

5

Glamorous and Gay Maharanis

For a vivid and true account of the lives and loves and intrigues of the Maharanis, Begums and Princesses of Indian States, I have made a selection from different regions of the North, East, West and South of India as a pattern and a replica of the mass of Maharanis, Begums and Princesses whose husbands went abroad and indulged in sex orgies with foreign women and neglected their consorts in India. Besides, most of these perverted Maharanis were the offspring of the ultra-modern education which they received under British tutors in India and at schools and colleges in England.

The Maharaja of Rajpipla, called PIP by his intimate friends, was most of the time in London with his British mistresses, and so were the Maharajas of other States like Kapurthala, Mandi, Baroda, Cooch-Behar, Palampur, Limdi, Bikaner, Jaipur and Indore.

I must express in unequivocal terms that I never found in my tours around the world more beautiful and refined women than the Maharanis, Begums and Princesses of India. Most of them came of the pure stock of old dynasties and claimed to be the descendants of Sun and Moon. It was a unique sight to see them in private social gatherings, bedecked with jewellery from head to toe. Their soft and sweet voices and their delicate ways of talking and walking were superb. Such a class of women does not exist today except in some Princely houses of Rajasthan, Punjab, Gujarat and Maharashtra. Maharani Gayatri Devi of Jaipur is the personification of beauty and charm. She reminds me of the attractive Eva Peron, wife of the former President of Argentina, who even after her death is worshipped in Argentina as a superhuman being.

Maharanis, Ranis, Begums and concubines have different status in the harem of Maharajas. The Maharanis were recognised as the legitimate wives of the Maharajas by the King of England, while the Ranis by tact, by hidden charm and by ruse, had to win the heart of the rulers to get to the status of the Maharanis. The offsprings of the Maharanis were the legitimate children of the Maharajas and were entitled to inheritance, while the children of the concubines and mistresses were not recognised.

Then there were different standards adopted for maintaining their positions. The senior Maharanis lived in gorgeous palaces while the Ranis and concubines had one or two rooms in the palaces allotted to them. There was differentiation in food, dress, jewellery, etc. Each woman was given food in accordance with her status. For instance, the Maharanis were served in gold plates. The number of dishes was fifty to seventy. Ranis ate in silver plates and the number of dishes ranged between 25 and 30. The concubines were served in copper plates and the dishes were between 10 and 15. The same difference existed when the Maharajas ordered clothes for them. Similar was the proportion of allotment of the members of staff for each Maharani, Rani and concubine at the palace.

There were picnics held in Mussoorie hills attended by men

and women from Indian aristocracy, British officials, both civil and military, and their womenfolk. Sumptuous lunches were taken in cars and special wagons to romantic picnic-spots. These picnic-spots were 10 to 15 miles away from Mussoorie in the higher regions of the Himalayas with rivulets flowing near the snow-clad summits. Wines and other alcoholic drinks were served to the participants. Usually, the Maharanis were the hostesses on these occasions. After lunch, the guests separated as couples by previous arrangements. There were special open-air decorative cloth enclosures without roofs, known as *'kanats'*, which gave seclusion to the occupants. The *'kanat'* is a piece of strong cloth in various colours hung round several poles pitched in the ground. Normally, there were four *'kanat'* on four sides to cover the place so that it became a special room for the guests to lie down and rest. Carpets were laid on the floor with multi-coloured cushions. Here some of the couples, both British and Indian, spent many hours resting before tea time. Generally, the guests reached there on horses or by rickshaws because the road was not motorable. It was in the knowledge of the guests assembled as to what happened inside the *'kanats'*. No one was inquisitive as all were in the same boat and complete confidence in one other prevailed. Many of the Maharajas whose Maharanis and Princesses came to these summer hill resorts were away in Europe with their British mistresses living in castles and mansions in London and Paris. Thus, these Maharanis and Princesses were quite free to spend their summer vacations unchecked and to have their sexual appetites fully satiated.

6

The Nawab's Dream Resort

Dumas was the capital of Sachin State in the west of India. The Ruler of Sachin, Nawab Hamidullah Khan, was very friendly with Maharaja Bhupinder Singh of Patiala, who was the Chancellor of the Chamber of Princes and the great and powerful Ruler of Patiala State in northern India. Hamidullah Khan wanted to develop Dumas as a seaside resort. He asked the Maharaja of Patiala to lend my services to him for a short while to plan the construction of Dumas as a holiday resort with a beautiful harbour and casino in the style of Monte Carlo and Las Vegas for the tourists from India and all over the world, a 5-star hotel, large roads and parks, and an additional harbour for passenger ships. I received a letter from Nawab Hamidullah Khan inviting me to Dumas.

I stayed at Dumas for some months, and as I had some experience of the construction of seaside resorts, watering places and casinos in Europe, I planned it as a beautiful tourist centre. Its cost in my estimate came to about twenty-five crores of rupees (equal to 250 million rupees). As the Nawab had no funds for such a venture, he asked some financiers from

Bombay to help him achieve his ambition. In the meantime, I was entertained by the Nawab in the most sumptuous way. Every evening he would get three chairs placed in a corner of his Palace Garden — Qusre Sultan, where the breeze flowed directly from the sea. These three chairs were reserved for the Nawab and his favourite Begum Naseem whom he called C in the fashion of some important rulers who had numerous wives who were named in alphabetic order or in numbers. The cool and lovely breeze from the tides and waves of the sea was most pleasant and refreshing. After enjoying the breeze for a short time and indulging in casual talk, the Nawab ordered alcoholic drinks to be served to the Begum and myself. We were the only two of the three to be participating in the delicious and intoxicating drinks. The Nawab himself abstained from drinking alcoholic beverages due to religious prejudices but he had no objection to his Begum sharing drinks with me. Usually, the Begum and I had many drinks before dinner was served at about 10 o'clock at night. At the dinner-table, there were French 'Champagne' and other white and red wines and liquors of all brands. After the dinner, the Nawab got himself excused and asked the Begum to continue to entertain me with drinks and her charming company till the late hours of the morning. The Begum was a most beautiful and charming Princess, of medium size with large eyes resembling those of a doe and an ivory complexion. She was about 27 years old and professed Muslim faith and belonged to a Muslim royal family. She wore gorgeous Muslim-style clothes with matching precious jewellery and her Urdu was stylish and chaste. I was entertained in this way for several weeks only at night as the Begum was in strict 'purdah' in daytime and I was not supposed to meet her.

When the Nawab and I went to Bombay to enlist the help of financiers, we stayed at the Taj Mahal Hotel where many dinner parties were given to which the Nawab invited the magnates of

Bombay for getting their financial help for building his casino. Sometimes the Nawab gave a dinner at the Willingdon Club, but before going there the guests would assemble first at Taj Mahal Hotel in his Royal Suite for drinks. It was then that the Nawab asked one of the business magnates to escort his Begum in his car to the Willingdon Club which is named after Earl of Willingdon, Viceroy of India. It is situated at a distance of about 10 Kms from the Taj Mahal Hotel. The Begum and the business magnate reached the Willingdon Club an hour later than the Nawab, the other guests and I had reached there. I was told later by the business magnate that the Begum was most cordial and loving to him on the way and he had one or two drinks with her at his own house before joining us at the Willingdon Club. The Begum and the magnate, whose name was Rahmat Fazal Bhai, were in a hilarious and gay mood when they reached the club. The Nawab seemed to accept the *'fait accompli'* willingly and such chivalrous behaviour of his guests towards his Begum did not cause a pang of jealousy in his heart or irritate him. The scheme was an excellent one and would have paid dividends if businessmen had invested money in it, but knowing the dictatorial powers which those Rulers enjoyed at that time in the States, it was difficult for the financiers from British India to invest money in a project like this, however profitable and tempting it might be. The Nawab later tried to raise money through the Princely Order, but there also he did not succeed in attracting his brother Princes to this tempting proposition. It was sheer bad luck of the Nawab and the country that such an alluring project did not materialise. Dumas would have been, as planned by me, another Monte Carlo, Cannes or Las Vegas, business benefits apart. Here is the original letter which I received from the Nawab of Sachin regarding the Junior Begum having an accident:

My dear Jarmani Dassji,

I do not remember if I have replied to your telegrams and letters yet. The Junior Begum (C) had a nasty accident nearly ten days ago and she had to be operated upon under chloroform. Since then I have nearly been driven mad with anxiety. So I know you will forgive my silence. I shall leave for Bombay on the 20th June afternoon.

More when we meet.

Sincerely,

Sd........

Later, the Nawab got so distressed due to the indisposition of the Begum that he gave up the project indefinitely. The Nawab was one of the most courteous and romantic rulers whom I met in my long service in the Indian states. His hospitality was unique and he did not even mind his Begum entertaining his personal and intimate guests with her charm and company at night ending with a game of Ping Pong a la Chinese.

7

Maharani Tara Devi's Tragic Romance

Tara Devi was a Czech beauty loved by Maharaja Jagatjit Singh of Kapurthala. He was the ruler of an important Sikh State in the Punjab, and enjoyed a 17-gun salute. He managed to include Tara Devi among his many Maharanis. She was the illegitimate daughter of a Hungarian count who had promised to marry her to his son through his legal wife. Then she met the Maharaja in Europe during his visit to Prague. With the help of her mother Madame Nina Grossup and grandmother Madame Pura Grossup, the Maharaja succeeded in persuading her to come to Kapurthala as his guest. The whole family came to Kapurthala in the usual way in which other European women used to come to India in the past, and were put up in the luxurious 'Louis XIV style' apartments of the Jagatjit Palace — the replica of Chateau de Versailles in France, the abode of Kings of France. The Maharaja presented her with precious jewels and magnificent dresses and after lavishly bestowing upon her such fine presents in cash and kind, asked her to marry him after she had lived with him for several months as his concubine. Her mother and grandmother advised her to accept the proposal of marriage by the Maharaja who afterwards travelled extensively with her in India and Europe. But Tara Devi soon got tired of the intrigues of the Palace, as her rise as a Maharani brought rivalries amongst the officials of the Palace of the State. To oust her from power, Sardar Mathura Dass, Private Secretary to the Maharaja and Mr. Sikand, Prime Minister of Kapurthala State, influenced the Maharaja against Tara Devi, her mother and her grandmother. The Maharani became tired of life due to these intrigues though she was having all luxuries in the way of food, dress, jewellery, accommodation, cars and honours. Her grandmother died at Mussoorie, followed by her mother, under mysterious circumstances which shocked Tara Devi. After the death of her mother and grandmother, she became disheartened and began to behave as if she had no interest in life. She began to refuse the visits of the Maharaja who tried his best to please her and spend a couple of nights in a week with her. She boldly refused to have any sexual relations with him and every time the Maharaja approached her for that purpose, she fainted at the thought that she would also meet the same fate as her mother and grandmother.

The Maharaja consulted Dr. M. Dass, his personal physician, and confided in him that he was unable to persuade the Maharani to have any sexual relations with him any longer. The doctor, who knew the physical disability of the Maharaja, told him bluntly that she was suffering from sexual hunger and as the Maharaja was unable to satisfy her sex desire, she had become allergic to the advances of the Maharaja.

The doctor suggested discreetly to the Maharaja that she should be sent out of Kapurthala with a young staff officer of her choice to recuperate her vitality and nerves. The Maharaja accepted the advice of the doctor reluctantly. He understood what the doctor meant. Soon afterwards Major Y. B. Singh accompanied her to Delhi for a short change and she with her staff officer stayed at the Maiden's Hotel. But by then her nerves had taken a turn for the worse, and she could not respond to the erotic advances of Major Singh.

One afternoon, Maharani Tara Devi hired a taxi to go to the Qutab Minar which is about 12 miles from the Maiden's Hotel where she was residing. On arriving there, she left the taxi. She then climbed to the highest point of the Qutab Minar and jumped from there and killed herself. Her body was found hanging on the railing of the second floor. That was the end of another love affair of the Maharaja. Tara Devi was buried in the cemetery at St. James' Church, Delhi, and the Maharaja erected a marble plaque on her tomb to perpetuate her memory and placed a wreath of flowers on her tomb whenever he visited Delhi. This was the last love affair of the Maharaja with an European woman.

8

Passionate Paswanji

His Highness Shri Himat Singhji, Dowlat Singhji, Maharaja of Idar, was a Rathor Rajput. He was born on the 2nd of October, 1899, and succeeded to the throne of Idar State on 14 April 1931. The capital of the State was Himatnagar. He enjoyed a 15-gun salute and full sovereign powers. He belonged to the same illustrious Rathor family as the Maharaja of Jodhpur. He accompanied his father, the late Maharaja Dowlat Singhji, to Europe where he went to attend the Coronation of His Majesty the King Emperor at London and acted as a page boy to His Imperial Majesty at the Coronation Durbar in 1911. Since then he had been visiting England every third or fourth year and mixing in the British society at London. It is true that he had developed a taste for British culture and British women.

However, he had a few setbacks with the fair sex in London and felt that he should have greater contact with Indian women. He went round searching for a suitable companion for himself. Ultimately, he found one Parsee girl by the name of Nargis and induced her to become his mistress.

With the lure of money and position, not much inducement was necessary as she had already had many lovers. He ultimately brought her to his palace and got her recognized by the State subjects as Paswanji, a status inferior to the legal wives of the Maharaja but having the semi-official recognition of a morganatic marriage. As the Maharaja was addicted to alcohol, he drank heavily every night. Paswanji became more and more powerful. She knew me intimately before she met the Maharaja and used to stay at my house 'Amaltas' at Kapurthala, though she was a guest of the Maharaja of Kapurthala and had a suite of rooms allotted to her at the Jagatjit Palace. Later, I introduced her to Himat Singhji Dowlat Singhji, who took her to Europe. While on his way back to India along with Paswanji on a P. & O. Liner, the Maharaja asked me to suggest to him a suitable person to be his Private Secretary. He imposed three conditions for the appointment as his Private Secretary: (i) he should be tall, (ii) he should be well-built, and (iii) he should be a graduate. As my nephew Rameshwar Dass fulfilled all these conditions, I suggested his name and the Maharaja readily appointed him as his Private Secretary on his return to India. Of course, Paswanji helped Rameshwar to be selected for this coveted post as he was a nephew of mine and Paswanji had full confidence in him.

After a few days, Paswanji left for Bombay to purchase some jewellery for the wedding of one of the relations of the Maharaja of Idar. She asked the Maharaja to allow Rameshwar Dass to accompany her to Bombay. Paswanji purchased jewellery worth lakhs of rupees and asked Rameshwar Dass to negotiate the price with the jewellers asking them to add 25 per cent to the bills as her share of the commission, out of which she promised to give Rameshwar 5 per cent. This she confided in Rameshwar as she was a friend of mine. This secret Rameshwar revealed to the Maharaja on his return to Himatnagar as his conscience revolted against it. The Maharaja asked Paswanji for an explanation about the accusations made by Rameshwar regarding the purchase of jewellery. Paswanji wept bitterly and fell at the feet of the Maharaja and pleaded that she was innocent and that Rameshwar was the villain and that he had concocted the story to malign her. After a few drinks of Scotch, the Maharaja began to fondle Paswanji and told her that he would never blame her of dishonesty. Rameshwar was summarily dismissed and asked to leave the State within five hours. His straightforwardness and loyalty to the Maharaja cost him the coveted position he was holding.

Rameshwar told me funny stories about the Maharaja who, after a few drinks of Scotch, would act like a beggar. He would put on torn and shabby clothes and worn-out shoes and put dust and ashes in his hair and go about with a begging bowl, shouting loudly: "I am a beggar, a poor man, and no food to eat for several days, have mercy on me and give me a coin." Courtiers, knowing the Maharaja's habit, gave 2, 4 and 8 anna pieces and sometimes a rupee according to their status. The Maharaja thanked all his donors in the same way as a poor man would do, saluting and blessing those who contributed for his food.

After a while, the affection of the Maharaja for Paswanji diminished and then she herself began to supply cheap English and Anglo-Indian women to the Maharaja. There were sumptuous parties in the Idar Palace in Bombay which were also attended by me and to which the Maharaja invited the Race Course gentry, jockeys and trainers and also persons of lower status. But members of higher society in Bombay and Poona never agreed to mix with her. The cultured and highly moral Parsee community to which she belonged discarded her.

The Maharaja of Idar had peculiar habits. After a few drinks, he used to call his military guards at 4 a.m. and ask them to parade before him. He used to give them command orders — March! Left, right, left, right.

The Aide-de-Camp in waiting commanded the guard to appear before the *durbar* as the Maharaja had called them. Then he would roll on the grass at 4 a.m. outside his palace in Poona and no one dared to ask him to return to his bedroom. Paswanji would beckon him to come inside but to no avail.

The Maharaja spent most of his time at races at Poona, Calcutta, Bombay and Bangalore, and he was in his own State only for a short time, to look after the administration.

Once when he was at Poona, the British Resident expressed a desire to see him. He got nervous and sent for his Chief Minister from Idar, the Capital, and shut himself in a room with Paswanji who was not allowed to appear at public functions arranged in honour of the Viceroy, the British Resident and other high-ranking officials of the Government of India.

Paswanji made herself quite rich not only by getting valuable gifts from the Maharaja but also by taking commissions and bribes from the jewellers and contractors for whom she secured business.

A lovable trait of Paswanji was that she never forgot her old lovers. Whenever there was an opportunity to be with them and share the bed with them, she never hesitated. As she had numerous lovers before she met the Maharaja of Idar, she always found time to express her past gratitude towards them by bestowing favours on them, that is, by offering herself.

Normally, the love affairs of Paswanji took place at Idar Palace in Bombay where she used to go alone every now and then to make purchases for the State. The Palace was safe and there was no danger that her infidelity to the Maharaja would be found out in that vast and secluded den of privacy.

9

Two Exotic Royal Sisters

Rani Madhvi of Jasdan was the wife of the Raja of Jasdan, Sardar Shri Ala Vajsuri, the former Ruler of a State in western India. Her daughter Gita is the Maharani of Kapurthala, married to the cultured and refined prince Maharaja Sukhjit Singh of Kapurthala who is at present serving as a colonel in the Indian Army. Rani Jasdan is one of the three beautiful daughters of Kanwar Gambhir Singh, a near relative of the Raja of Jubbal, a State in the Himalayas. Her eldest sister was Princess Brinda of Kapurthala who was married to His Highness Maharaja Paramjit Singh of Kapurthala. But she died before Paramjit Singh became Maharaja after the death of his father and thus never assumed the title of Maharani.

His Highness Jagatjit Singh, the father of Paramjit Singh, was fond of French language and culture. He asked Kanwar Gambhir Singh to betroth his eldest daughter Brinda to the heir-apparent of the State. This proposal Gambhir Singh immediately accepted. As the family was in dire financial difficulties, it was a boon to Gambhir Singh to have such a matrimonial alliance for his daughter with the heir-apparent of Kapurthala. But

Gambhir Singh fell out on this issue with the Raja of Jubbal as the Raja was opposed to Brinda's marriage to the future ruler of Kapurthala State. This was due to caste prejudice because he considered himself to be a Rajput of pure blood. He despised the family of Kapurthala, which was descended from the low caste of wine-sellers. The girl Brinda was immediately taken to the Palace at Kapurthala and later to Paris where she stayed with Princess Amede de Broglie (who belonged to one of the noblest families of France) as her guest. Within a short time Brinda started speaking French and English fluently and turned out to be a cultured and Europeanised modern girl. On her return from Paris, she was married to Paramjit Singh with great pomp and show in the newly-built Jagatjit Palace at Kapurthala, and the marriage was attended by the representatives of the King Emperor, important Maharajas of India, and hundreds of Indian and European guests. Princess Amede de Broglie and several other French friends of the Maharaja came to Kapurthala from Paris to participate in the marriage celebrations and to witness and enjoy oriental splendour and hospitality. While important and distinguished guests were put up in different palaces, others were accommodated in a huge camp in the extensive park of the Palace in several rows of dining and living tents. When chandeliers in crystal glass were lit at night, it looked like a fairy land.

Brinda gave birth to four daughters one after the other, and as the Maharaja was anxious to have a son to succeed to the throne of Kapurthala, he advised his son Paramjit Singh to marry again. He selected a princess of the noble Rajput family for his son's consort, from whom a son was born and baptised in the Sikh religion and named Sukhjit Singh. The relations between Paramjit Singh and Brinda had been strained for a long time, so that both took to different paths of life.

Brinda by her haughty temperament had become unpopular among the officials of the State as well as among the relatives of the Maharaja. She was given a handsome allowance from the state exchequer and a beautiful villa four miles from the Kapurthala Palace on the bank of the river Bein. She went to France, North and South America and other countries and stayed with her European and American friends for long periods. As there were no restrictions on her movements, she could go out of Kapurthala and return as she pleased; neither the Maharaja nor the heir-apparent were interested in her any more.

I do not want to enter into her personal life in the U.S.A. and South American countries with the gigolos and pleasure-seekers. But I thought she could have done some useful work in India with the education and culture she had, instead of spending her time in merry-making in the capitals of the world and spending away all the money she received from the exchequer.

Brinda is another glaring example of women brought up and educated in Europe who become useless burdens. She did come back to India and live in her villa at Kapurthala for a short time, but ultimately she went to America and settled down there.

Madhvi used to live permanently at Kapurthala with her sister Brinda, and her two brothers, Kanwar Mohinder Singh and Kanwar Rajinder Singh, had nicknamed her Kaju before she got married to the Raja of Jasdan. Madhvi was very friendly with many officials of the State, particularly with Sardar Bharpur Singh, Private Secretary to the heir-apparent, her brother-in-law. Many romantic conversations between Madhvi and Sardar Bharpur Singh were heard by me on the telephone in my office at the Palace of Kapurthala. It was pleasant to hear them talk in such amorous whispers. Later she married Sardar Shri Khachar Ala Vajaur of Jasdan who succeeded to the Gaddi on 11 June 1919.

He was invested with full powers of Talluka, governed by the rule of primogeniture, a departure from the usual Kati custom which provides for equal division of inheritance. He enjoyed unlimited civil powers except that the State could not try persons other than its own subjects for capital offences and provided that sentences of death required confirmation of the Hon'ble Agent to the Governor-General, Western Indian States.

Rani Madhvi, somehow or other, could not pull on with the Raja of Jasdan as he had a wife before he married Madhvi and from whom he had a son who was declared heir-apparent of Jasdan State. She left Jasdan and started living at Sunder Nagar, New Delhi. For two decades there were constant disputes between the Raja and the senior Rani. Later, she got legally separated from the Raja.

The only time the Raja of Jasdan came to Delhi was when his refined daughter Gita from Madhvi was married to Sukhjit Singh of Kapurthala. Being crippled by paralysis, he was brought to the hotel on a stretcher to attend the marriage of his daughter. I was also invited to this wedding and the reception at the Ashoka Hotel to which more than a thousand guests were invited. It was a pitiable sight to see Raja Jasdan in this dilapidated physical condition while Madhvi was gay and jolly. She was seen entertaining her Nepalese friends to her heart's content. Some guests pointed out to me that Nepalese friends were her latest craze. In her younger days, she was friendly with a French jeweller, Monsieur Andre Schoff, who gave her precious jewels as gifts. The Raja of Jasdan was miserable at the fag end of his life and was neglected by his Ranis. He was incapacitated due to paralysis and died after a protracted illness.

10

Eros in Matriarchy

Sir C.P. Ramaswamy Iyer was a great scholar, reformer and statesman of repute. As the Diwan of Travancore for many years, he brought about big reforms. He abolished the traditional custom of women untying brassieres from their breasts when seeing the Maharaja, Diwan or a Brahmin. It is a common and popular story in Trivandrum that whenever Sir C.P. appeared in the presence of women whose breasts were not covered, they lifted up their skirts to cover their breasts to obey the orders of the Diwan.

Sir C.P. was impelled to pass this order by the Viceroy of India and the King of England who received complaints from the Christian population that, against their culture and religion, they had to leave their breasts uncovered in the presence of the dignitaries. The Viceroy of India and the King of England saw justification in the complaint of the Christians of Travancore.

During the minority of the Maharaja, Maharani Sethu Lakshmibai was Regent of the State. According to the matriarchal system, the Maharaja's mother was not to become the Regent, but his father's sister had a prior claim. Sir C.P. Ramaswamy was also for many years a member of the Executive Council of the Viceroy of India and wielded great power and influence with Lady Willingdon, the Vicereine of India whom he addressed by her Christian name. I used to see him sometimes at Hotel Imperial, New Delhi, where he usually stayed, and heard him talking on the telephone to Lady Willingdon with whom he had long, loving conversations from his hotel suite.

Maharani Sethu Parvathi Bai, mother of the Maharaja of Travancore, was a well-known beauty. Sir C.P. Ramaswamy Iyer came to Trivandrum to plead an important judicial case on behalf of the Christian Association and met Maharani Regent Sethu Lakshmibai in his official capacity as a counsel of his clients. Sir C.P. fell in love with Maharani Parvathi Bai at first sight and later, with the help of the Viceroy of India, managed to get himself appointed as Diwan of Travancore. It was customary in all important States that the appointment of the Diwan should be approved by the Viceroy of India as the representative of the paramount power.

Maharani Parvathi Bai responded to the ardent love of Sir C.P. and soon the Maharani and Sir C.P. reciprocated each other's love with great passion — so much so that their love affair became the talk of the whole State and the political circles in the Viceroy's house. But as the Diwan was powerful and the mother of the Maharaja wielded great influence and prestige in the royal family and the nobles of the State, nobody dared raise a finger of protest.

But the people of the State soon got disgusted with the open exhibition of the immoral relationship of C.P. with the Maharani and with the palace intrigues, and he became most unpopular. His bona fides were suspected, when he declared the independence of Travancore State without consulting the young ruler. The people of the state demanded his dismissal forthwith, but as he had the unflinching support of the mother of the Maharaja, he stuck to his post till he was assaulted by an assailant who made an attempt on his life. C.P. escaped with cuts on his nose and lips and then left clandestinely for fear of losing his life. The Maharaja accepted the integration of the State after his visit to Sardar Vallabhbhai Patel, Union Home Minister in Delhi, whom he told that until his god Padmanabhan permitted him to integrate his State with India, he would not agree to the integration. It is said that Sardar Patel told the Maharaja that he would consult Lord Padmanabhan about this important matter in his prayer room on behalf of the Maharaja. He came out of the prayer room after a few minutes and told the Maharaja that Lord Padmanabhan had agreed that the State of Travancore should be integrated with India. The Maharaja, having no excuse left, voluntarily signed the documents regarding the integration of Travancore then and there.

Sir C.P. Ramaswamy Iyer represented Travancore State at the two sessions of the Round Table Conference in London.

Maharani Sethu Parvathi Bai, Sir C.P. Ramaswamy Iyer and I travelled by a P. & O. liner while returning to India after the session of the first Round Table Conference. I noticed that Sir C.P. and the Maharani had three or four suites of cabins adjacent to each other and this contained large bedrooms and drawing rooms. As a matter of fact, one corner of the liner was reserved for the Maharani of Travancore and Sir C.P.. No secrecy was observed by them and the Maharani and Sir C.P. were found embracing each other, strolling on the deck, or having drinks in their open rooms. As nobody bothered as to what the other passengers were doing, Sir C.P. and the Maharani were carrying on their amorous game openly. Their love affair was known to the passengers on the steamer and it did not matter to them if they were talked about in whispers.

On return to Travancore, Maharani Parvathi Bai continued to stay with her son, the Maharaja of Travancore, in the Kawadiar Palace which was frequently visited by Sir C.P. As the Maharaja was a minor, there was no check on the amorous game of Sir C.P. and Maharani Parvathi Bai.

Travancore was an important State in the South and the Maharaja His Highness Padmanabh Dasa Vanchi Pala Sir Rama Verma Kulasekhara Kiritapati Manney Sultan Maharaja Raja Ramraja Bahadur Sham Shemsherjang C.C.I. Maharaja of Travancore enjoyed a 10-gun salute.

Travancore was the southern-most of Indian States and occupied the south-west portion of the Indian Peninsula. It was bounded on the north by the State of Cochin and the District of Coimbatore.

The ruler of the State belonged to the Kshatriya family which traces its descent to the ancient Chera Kings of south India. The old principal town of Tiruvankodu which gave its name to the State is now a small town.

The ruling family follows the ancient Marumakathayan law or the law of inheritance through the female line. A special *sanad* by Earl Canning authorised the right of adoption to perpetuate the dynasty. In 1900, Sethu Lakshmibai and Sethu Parvathi Bai were adopted as Ranis of Attingal. The title Maharani was conferred on them on September 1924. The Senior Maharani was married in May 1906 to Ram Varma, a nephew of the later Kerala Verma Valiakoil Tanpuran and Maharani Parvathi Bai was married to Ravi Verma, a member of the Kolliamanur family, in April 1907. The heir-apparent bears the title of Elaya Raja. The Senior Maharani gave birth to two daughters on 30 December 1923 and the 3rd October 1926 respectively. Her Highness Maharani Sethu Parvathi Bai had two sons and a daughter born on 17 September

1916. The sons born on 17 November 1912 was called the 'Maharaja' and the other born on the 22nd March 1922 was called the 'Elaya Raja'. Karthika Thirumal, sister of His Highness the Maharaja, was married in January 1934 to Goda Varma Raja, a member of the Poonjar family. The title of 'Her Highness' was formally conferred only on the Senior Rani of Attingal and in March 1933 the title of 'Her Highness' was also conferred upon the mother of the ruler of Travancore though she was not the Senior Maharani.

11

Dividing the Rulers
Not the Ruled

During British Rule in India, the Mysore State was the most progressive State with a proper constitution and a legislature composed of elected members who were to lay down policies for the State. His Highness Krishna Raja Wadiyar of Mysore was a ruler of saintly disposition and enjoyed the goodwill, love and admiration of his subjects. He was considered an ideal ruler, but it was his Diwan who actually ruled the State on account of the Maharaja's attitude of 'laissez-faire' which left the administration of the State in the hands of the Diwan. He had many able Diwans and administrators, such as Dr. M. Visvesvaraya, one of India's greatest engineers, Sir Albion Banerjee and his last Diwan, Sir Mirza Mohammed Ismail. All these Diwans wielded tremendous power and had their own way in administering the State, so much so that the Maharaja was reduced to a figurehead under the guise of a constitutional monarch. The Diwan, under cover of the Legislature, wielded power as if there were no Constitution and no Legislature. Many important laws were enacted and even at the height of glory of the British power, Mysore was considered to be a State administered on democratic principles where the voice of the people was heard, though it was often drowned by the dictatorial attitude and powers of the Diwan.

Sir Mirza Ismail was a shrewd politician whom I had the pleasure of knowing very closely. We were together during the sessions of the Round Table Conference at London. We also spent some time together sightseeing in gay Paris. In later years I often met him at Mysore, Bangalore, Jaipur and Delhi. He ruled the State with an iron hand for over 15 years, and as he had supreme control over the administration and did not brook any interference from the Maharaja or any member of the royal family, he became a virtual dictator. His pet hobby was to beautify Mysore and Bangalore with roads and buildings, and he followed the same pattern of beautification in the capitals of other States as well, such as Jaipur, where he was later appointed Prime Minister. He turned the city of Jaipur, called the Pink City due to the pink colour of its buildings, into a picturesque city with properly laid boulevards and avenues and had the main street named after himself.

The city of Bangalore was frequented by British officers, both civilian and military, in large numbers. The Dussera Festival in Mysore was a unique event which attracted tourists not only from India but also from abroad. On this great occasion, the Palace of Mysore, the principal buildings and the roads as well as the Chamundi Temple on the Hill were illuminated. The Maharaja, dressed in gorgeous attire and bedecked in jewellery, rode on an elephant to the festive ceremonies where the great Lord Rama was to kill Ravana, the ogre King of Lanka. State troops, military bands, both Indian and European and orchestra, were on attendance. At night a huge banquet was held in which both Europeans and Indians participated. Bands with Indian musical instruments such as the Jal Tarang were playing as well as the Indian State Band.

Bangalore was a city of gaiety and romance. The British men and women collected there during the season to participate in the races, balls, and other gay functions, and it is there that the Princes of the royal family of Mysore got to know the British women intimately. As I said before, it was in this period of Indian history that British women mixed with the Princes and their Ministers and staff officers without any formality and restraint, and love affairs between them were common.

The Maharaja had no son to succeed him. However, he had a brother, Prince K.N.R. Wadiyar, whom the Maharaja proclaimed as his heir-apparent and gave the title of Yuvaraja of Mysore. The British Government recognised K.N.R. Wadiyar as the next in succession and conferred upon him the exalted order of the Grand Cross of the Indian Empire of His Majesty the King Emperor of India.

The Yuvaraja, being young and handsome, attracted the attention of British women. He got used to their company and charm, and started visiting England to meet them and their friends. These visits of the Yuvaraja to England often gave Sir Mirza Ismail opportunities to rule the State according to his will as the Yuvaraja was the only person who could thwart the plans of the Diwan if they were not rightly directed towards the welfare of the people and the State. He, therefore, encouraged the Yuvaraja to go often to Europe, and provided him larger amounts of money than were necessary for his expenses in foreign countries. Whenever the Yuvaraja returned from Europe, he meddled with the affairs of the State. This displeased Sir Mirza and he tried to drive a wedge between the Maharaja and the Yuvaraja by relating to the Maharaja some false stories about the conduct of the Yuvaraja in foreign countries.

I was in Europe in those days when the Yuvaraja visited London, Paris and other capitals of Europe. I had first-hand information on how the Yuvaraja behaved. He behaved like any respectable man with the pride of Princely descent. He did not squander money on women and wine like other Princes who were in Paris or other capitals of Europe at that time.

Whenever the Yuvaraja returned to India, his relations with the Maharaja became more and more lukewarm.

On his return to India after his last trip to Europe, the Yuvaraja stayed at Bombay in a house called "The Anchorage" on Strand Street at the Apollo Bunder. He invited me to spend a couple of weeks with him. I stayed at the Cricket Club of India and paid the bills of the Club from my own pocket, as I did not want to burden him with the payment of these bills, his financial position at that time being rather bad. The Diwan refused to pay even the doctor's bills and his air passage.

In a letter, the Yuvaraja complained about this to the Secretary of State for India. He was negotiating with some jewellers to sell his jewels, including a valuable necklace which was an heirloom. I saw the Yuvaraja daily. He was sane and in perfect control of himself though he had developed some heart trouble with oedema and anemia, due to tension and the friction he was having with his brother, the Maharaja of Mysore, and due to the intrigues of Sir Mirza Ismail. He opened his heart to me and showed me certain letters which he had received from his brother, one of which is reproduced as Annexure 1.

Having no hope of redress from his brother, he asked me to represent his case to Sir Bertrand Glancy, the Political Secretary, and to the Viceroy of India, to Mahatma Gandhi and other Congress leaders. While I was at Bombay, he showed me some letters in which it was clearly stated by some eminent doctors of London and Bombay that the Yuvaraja was not insane as alleged by his brother the Maharaja of Mysore at the instigation of his

Diwan. Letters from the doctors in Bombay are reproduced as Annexures 2 and 3. He also showed me a very important letter His Highness Sir Sultan Mohammed Shah, Aga Khan the Great, had written to his brother saying how the behaviour of the Yuvaraja in the capitals of Europe was praiseworthy and how he was acting as a good ambassador of his country in creating a good impression on the Europeans about the rulers of India and their heirs-apparent.

The letter of the Aga Khan is reproduced as Annexures 4 and 5.

When an exalted personage like the Aga Khan had written to the Maharaja about the conduct of his brother, the Yuvaraja, in such glowing terms, the Maharaja ought to have changed his attitude towards the Yuvaraja. But he listened to the advice of the Diwan who had become more and more hostile to the Yuvaraja. The Diwan did not want the relationship between the Maharaja and his brother to be cordial as it would then interfere with his plans to rule the State in accordance with his own wishes.

In his own lifetime, the Yuvaraja was told that he was no longer the heir-apparent and that his son Prince Jaya Chama Raja would succeed his uncle as the Maharaja of Mysore after his death. Prince Jaya Chama Raja Wadiyar succeeded as Maharaja of Mysore and became the most renowned Maharaja. After the integration of the State, he became Raj Pramukh and later was appointed Governor of Mysore State and Madras State. He is a great scholar and a man of letters, and is loved by the people of the State.

The Yuvaraja of Mysore sought legal advice as to whether the Maharaja could adopt his son as the successor, and the legal opinion of an eminent lawyer (which is quoted below) was that, according to Hindu Law, the Maharaja could not adopt his son without his approval and consent, particularly when the Yuvaraja had no other sons to perform the rites of his father after his death.

When I saw the Yuvaraja of Mysore at Bombay, he was broken-hearted and refused to go to Mysore. He knew that he would be ill-treated and not received by the Maharaja or the Diwan in accordance with the status and position of the heir-apparent of the State.

As mentioned above, the Yuvaraja asked me to plead his case with the Government of India and with Mahatma Gandhi. He authorised me in writing to take any action I thought fit. On arrival at Delhi, I asked for an interview with the Viceroy of India and the Political Secretary. I planned to see Mahatma Gandhi also. Before I could see any of them, I heard on the radio at the Imperial Hotel, where I was staying, that the Yuvaraja of Mysore had expired. This news grieved me deeply.

Out of malice, the body of the Yuvaraja was cremated at Bombay and not taken to Mysore as should have been the case when the heir-apparent of a big State like Mysore died. Further, to add insult to injury, his coffin made of wood was intentionally made shorter than the full length of his body and, to the disgust of the public, his feet were seen hanging out when the funeral procession was taken out. However, his ashes were buried in a mausoleum in Mysore with due honours. Thus the Yuvaraja of Mysore, a talented Prince and statesman of vision, expired under mysterious circumstances. I went to Ootacamund to offer my condolences to the Yuvaraja's son and to relate to him the glorious past of his father.

The British officials in India were playing into the hands of Sir Mirza Ismail and acting in accordance with his whims. As I stated in my book *Maharaja*, the Prime Ministers of the States acted as the stooges of the Viceroy and the political department and, in return, they were given immense powers to perpetuate the rule of the Emperor of India (The King of England had the title of Emperor of India). The protocol in the Durbars and Receptions followed the same lines as those in the time of the Mughal Emperor.

When King George V came to India and held the Durbar in 1911 at Delhi to celebrate his coronation, the rulers were asked to pay homage to their sovereign. Certain rules were framed as to how they should pay their homage to the Emperor who was seated on the gilded royal throne on a high pedestal. The rulers had to bow before him and retrace seven steps facing the Emperor before turning round to resume their seats. This was most humiliating to the rulers who proclaimed themselves to be the descendants of the Sun and the Moon and of Lord Rama and Lord Krishna.

The episode of His Highness the Maharaja Sayaji Rao Gaekwad of Baroda when he presented himself before the King is too well-known all over India and abroad to be repeated here. Instead of taking a bejewelled sword in his hand and decorating himself with jewels and decorations like the other Maharajas, he went in a simple white coat and loose trousers with the turban on his head. He carried a light wooden stick with which he saluted the King. This irked the King very much. When the film taken on this occasion was shown at the Scala Theatre in London, the Maharaja was shouted upon as a traitor, the spectators yelling, "Hang the traitor! Depose him!" There was uproar in the hall and it was with great difficulty that calm and order were restored.

Thus the British Government ruled the Indian States with puppet Ministers who snatched power from the hands of the Rulers and reduced them to mere figureheads.

ANNEXURE 1

The Palace
Mysore
21ˢᵗ February 40

My dear Brother,

I have received from Colonel Gordon a copy of your letter to him of the 4ᵗʰ instant in which you have made certain complaints of the way in which you have been treated in respect of the matter of your return to India and I feel that I must make one more effort to arrive at a better understanding with you.

You seem from your letter to have an idea that the treatment that was accorded to you in England was dictated by me and by your friends on this side. I want to assure you in the first instance that that is not at all the true state of the case. Far from it.

I will not refer to our unfortunate difference of opinion as to the propriety of your taking your family to Europe at all at a time when the war clouds were gathering overt the world. My fears have been only too unhappily fulfilled. It has been a still greater source of grief to me that from quite an early stage of your tour your conduct had become a matter of unfavourable comment — a scandal — if I may use the word employed by friends in Europe, so that before you arrived in England, the Secretary of State and Viceroy were in receipt of reports from the Embassies regarding your behaviour. Your arrival in England coincided with your dispute with the Hollimd-America line, of which I need say no more than that the Secretary of State guaranteed the payment after a full consideration of all the facts, including the fact that the good name of the Mysore State was involved owing to your behaviour during your stay at the Hague. Then came the immediate question of securing the safe return of your family, for which I had to provide as you had failed to do so. Thereafter I received a succession of letters and telegrams from the authorities and from our old friends in England urging that you be required to return as your conduct was causing much adverse comment, and that a medical man be sent with you as you were ceasing to be responsible for your actions. The same has continued since your arrival in Bombay.

You complain especially of restrictions being placed on your handling of your money and securities. I must remind you of your position and mine in respect of the portion of the tax-payers' money that is entrusted to us for the maintenance of our position and dignities. We are not like private persons in this matter. We are members of the Princely Order, and the Princely Order is under a searchlight. You have spent in a few short months over ten lakhs of rupees. Instances of your reckless expenditure are being published abroad, while I hear of suggested speculations and other enterprises that I cannot think you have entered into with a full understanding of what they involve. Meanwhile, I have received medical opinion that you are not mentally in a condition to control your affairs. It is inevitable in these circumstances that some restrictions should be placed upon you and that you should not be allowed to convert the securities that stand in your name for the purposes that you have specified.

My object in writing this letter is not to reproach you but to beg of you to send away the people by whom you are surrounded, to give up your ambitious schemes, to restrict your expenditure within moderate limits, and above all, to conduct yourself in a manner worthy of your position.

It gave me, as it must have given to all our friends, intense pain to read of the happenings in a theatre recently in Bombay. So you really think that any sensible man would have put himself in such a humiliating position?

Indeed I should not be surprised. I fully expected it if the Bombay Government were to take steps to have you removed from Bombay, as the British Government did from England.

I do not insist upon your returning to Mysore. You may do as you like. But I must still ask you to keep your expenditure within reasonable limits, to send away all but your personal staff and so to regulate your conduct that there may be no complaints from the authorities or from your neighbours. You are becoming the subject of public talk everywhere.

I hope you will receive this letter in the spirit in which it is written.

Yours ever

Sd: Krishna Raja Wadiyar

ANNEXURE 2

K.R. Khosla,
L.A.A. (London)
F.R.C.A. (Glasgow)
Barrister-at-Law

6 A, Curzon Road,
New Delhi
Dated the 29ᵗʰ January 1940

To
Diwan Jarmani Dass,
Imperial Hotel,
New Delhi

Subject: The case of His Highness the Yuvaraja of Mysore:

My dear Diwan Sahib,

With reference to the conversation you had with me on the subject, I understand from the facts stated by you that the Yuvaraja Sahib is seeking advice on the following points:

(a)   The custody and control of his children without any interference on the part of His Highness the Maharaja of Mysore.

(b)   Full control of the operations of his personal estate, finances, securities and investments which are his personal property, and in regard

to which he is entitled to deal with and dispose of at his own discretion and without the intervention of anybody in the management thereof as apart from his own wishes.

(c) To claim arrears of pension as due to him under a scheme brought about by Sir K. Seshadri Aiyer in the year 1890 and sanctioned by the Governor General in Council on the 20th of August 1893.

(d) A proper adjustment of accounts of his personal property in accordance to his benefit.

With regard to (a) I am of the opinion that His Highness the Maharaja of Mysore can have no rights to the custody or guardianship of the children of Yuvaraja Sahib in the absence of a mutual agreement between Yuvaraja Sahib and His Highness the Maharaja of Mysore.

In the event of His Highness the Maharaja of Mysore contemplating an adoption of the eldest son of Yuvaraja Sahib, I am of the opinion that this cannot be done either under the Dharma Shastra or any other custom. As for the guardianship, the father is the natural guardian and unless any unfitness to the detriment of the children can be proved against the father such guardianship cannot be eliminated. Consequently, I maintain that Yuvaraja Sahib is fully entitled to the custody, control and guardianship of his children in every respect.

(b) There is no doubt that under the Hindu Law, His Highness the Maharaja of Mysore is the rightful Trustee and "Karta" of the estate of the Joint Hindu Family, but as soon as a certain amount is definitely allocated to the share of an individual member of the family that member becomes the full owner of that apportioned part of the estate and is fully entitled to operate, control, dispose of and manage the same in any manner he may choose to do. Such dealings and operations are entirely outside the jurisdiction of the "Karta" of the family and no interference can be enforced by him contrary to the wishes and control of the member of the family whom the estate has been apportioned and given to.

(c) There is no doubt that the pension of rupees one lakh and fifty

thousand is allotted to the apparent successor to the throne, and as long as the Yuvaraja Sahib holds the position of Heir-Apparent, he is fully entitled to receive the full amount of rupees one lakh and fifty thousand per annum.

(d) Inasmuch as the Comptroller is entrusted with the proper administration of the account entrusted to him, and is therefore a Trustee Administrator of the estate of Yuvaraja Sahib. As such the Comptroller is certainly liable to administer the estate of Yuvaraja Sahib in accordance to the wishes of Yuvaraja Sahib, and is fully liable to render account to Yuvaraja Sahib, and explain any defalcation or wrongful adjustment, if any. As a Trustee he may be found guilty of breach of trust in the event if any misfeasance or intentional default in the discharge of his functions of office.

All these matters require a serious approach to His Highness Maharaja Sahib of Mysore and to the Government of India, if necessary and I am sure an amicable settlement of all these matters can be safely brought about by a proper handling of the case.

Please note that I have charged you a very paltry sum of rupees two thousand for this consultation. I shall be glad if you will kindly arrange to let me have a cheque for the same at your earliest convenience.

In the event of His Highness the Yuvaraja Sahib deciding to hand over this brief to me, my fees for such retention of services will be rupees twenty thousand exclusive of all out-of-pocket expenses and irrespective of the amount of work to be involved in the case.

Yours sincerely

Sd: K.R. Khosla

ANNEXURE 3

"The Anchorage"
Strand Road
Bombay
6ᵗʰ March 1940

My dear Sir Bertrand,

As you know I arrived in India from Europe, and I am at present staying on here for medical treatment. If my health permits, I would like to come to Delhi to see you, and some of my friends in Rajputana and Northern India, by whom I am invited. In the meantime, I am sending a personal, verbal message to you through Diwan Jarmani Dass who would submit to you on my behalf certain matters with are of vital importance to me and my children.

I shall be most grateful if you will kindly give favourable consideration to what will be conveyed to you on my behalf, by Diwan Jarmani Dass. I am in need of your valuable advice.

Lots of false reports against me seem to have been spread by some interested people. Unless I am given opportunity to explain matters, it will be a one-sided story based on misrepresentation of facts.

I hope that you and Lady Glancy are quite well.

With best regards,

Yours very sincerely

....

From His Highness the Yuvaraja of Mysore, G.C.I.E.
To
The Honourable Sir Bertrand Glancy, K.C.S.I.
Political Adviser to His, Excellency
*   The Crown Representative*

ANNEXURE 4

Land's End
Malabar Hill
Bombay
5th March 1940

My dear Yuvaraja,

I am herewith sending you a copy of the letter which I sent to your brother for your perusal.

I hope you are better.

With kindest regards,

Yours very sincerely
Sd: Aga Khan

ANNEXURE 4 B

Copy of the letter sent to His Highness the Maharaja of Mysore, by His Highness the Aga Khan.

Land's End,
Malabar Hill
Bombay
5th March 1940

My dear Maharaja Sahib,

I am just writing this letter to say that when I passed through Italy on my way to India, the Italians were praising His Highness the Yuvaraja of Mysore as a cultured Prince and were saying that no other Indian Prince had before impressed them more with his personality and musical entertainments than the Yuvaraja of Mysore.

I *congratulate Your Highness and the Yuvaraja for the great service which the Yuvaraja rendered to Mysore and India in bringing such a happy understanding between the East and the West and for creating such an excellent impression about Indian culture and civilisation in Europe during his last visit there.*

I *thought you would perhaps like to hear what your brother has been doing in Europe during his travels and so I have written this letter.*

I *hope you are enjoying excellent health.*

With best regards,

Yours very sincerely

. . . .

ANNEXURE 5

Copy of Cablegram

D.L.T.

To
Colonel Neale
India Office
London

Mysore Palace debiting aeroplane and Doctor Macbridge's fees to my account kindly as promised speak to Secretary of State and cable Viceroy advising authorities to see the amount is not debited to my account and thus save my financial ruin.

Yuvaraja

4-3-40

ANNEXURE 6

Copy

Grosvenor House
24, Mayo Road
Bombay
24th February 1940

STATEMENT

H.H. The Yuvaraja of Mysore has been known to me since 17th Feb. 1940 and has been under my treatment for 5 days. He is suffering from heart trouble with oedema, and an anemia of the miscrocytic type.

During the time when I attended to H.H., we had many talks about medical and other subjects, and I found that, in his conversations, he showed a very high intellectual standard. I cannot understand how some people come to the conclusion that H.H. should not be mentally fit. On H.H.'s request I state that my personal experience with him has not given me the slightest proof for this assumption.

Sd: A. H. Starn

ANNEXURE 7

I have examined His Highness The Yuvaraja of Mysore and I have come to the conclusion that he is suffering from myocardial damage due to coronary sclerosis with symptoms of congestive cardiac failure. His Highness is also suffering from an enlarged cirrohosed liver.

Regarding treatment in my opinion the most important item is rest physical and mental and the physical rest should be absolute in bed.

I have been asked to pronounce an opinion regarding His Highness' mental state. I can definitely say that, his mental state is quite sound.

Sd: P.C. Bharucha
M.D. (London)

12

Maharani as a Boy

It was with great difficulty that Lord Curzon of Kedleston allowed His Highness Maharaja Jagatjit Singh of Kapurthala to go to Europe. But he was not permitted to take any of his Maharanis with him. However, with the help and advice of my father Diwan Daulat Ram, who had become his chief advisor after his return from London where he was called to the Inner Temple and became a full-fledged Barrister-at-Law, the Maharaja manipulated to take with him to Europe one of his young Maharanis named Kanari whom the Maharaja loved very much. Since she could not go to Europe as a Maharani, she accompanied him disguised as a Sikh boy dressed in *achkan* and trousers with a turban as her headgear. As there was no passport system in those days, she travelled with him disguised as a boy unnoticed by the Government officials in India and Europe. The Maharaja and Maharani enjoyed their stay in Europe. When there was nobody to watch her, she dressed herself as a woman in the apartments reserved for her by the Maharaja in hotels and chateaus in France. The Maharaja and Maharani were the guests of the French nobility who were in the know of the secret and were assumed to keep up the confidence reposed in them by the Maharaja. Maharani Kanari was one of the most beautiful and elegant women belonging to the noble families of Rajputs in Kangra district. She gave birth to a boy and a girl. Her son was Maharaj Kumar Karamjit Singh who grew into a handsome and cultured prince. The daughter was Maharaj Kumari Amrit Kaur who got married to His Highness Raja Joginder Sen of Mandi, the ruler of an important State in Himachal Pradesh in the Himalayas. After the integration of the States and the independence of India, Raja Joginder Sen was appointed Ambassador of India in Brazil where he performed his duties to the satisfaction of the Government of India. I was present at the wedding of Maharaj Kumari Amrit Kaur with Raja Joginder Sen at Kapurthala on the 4th, 5th and 6th February 1923. The wedding ceremony festivities were grand and they were attended by His Excellency the Governor of the Punjab and Lady Maclagan and other distinguished personalities of India including many Maharajas, Maharanis, Princesses, Ministers and notables of the States and of British India. The Raja was taken in a procession on a gorgeously caparisoned elephant from the Kapurthala Station to the Palace where he was to be put up. Besides luncheons, dinners and banquets, a torchlight tattoo and fireworks were held in front of the Palace. The poor were fed in thousands and were given cash presents. Maharaj Kumari Amrit Kaur gave birth to a son nicknamed Tibu, the heir-apparent of the State, who turned out to be a handsome and educated prince but his mother took to alcoholic drinks to which her mother Maharani Kanari was addicted. She left for the U.S.A. where she stayed for many years alone and later separated from her husband, the Raja of Mandi. The latter then married the daughter of Sardar Pinki, a nobleman and close relative of His Highness the Maharaja of Rajpipla.

Amrit Kaur died in the U.S.A. in dire pecuniary conditions. That was the end of the Princess who was brought up by her father in great luxury. Her Western education had turned her head and brought her to a miserable end.

After many months of stay in European capitals, Maharaja and Maharani Kanari returned to India and landed at Bombay where they were received by the Military Secretary of the Governor of Bombay on behalf of the Viceroy of India. But the Maharani remained un-noticed as she was dressed up like a boy. This showed how the Maharajas at that time were shrewd enough to hoodwink the Viceroy and the officials of the Government of India and how they managed to live according to their own whims and fancies.

13

When Jinnah Pleaded
for an Adulteress

The love affair of Maharaja Jagatjit Singh of Kapurthala with a
Spanish beauty, Anita Delgado of Spain, was a romantic topic
in the societies of Spain, France and India. The romance had
its beginnings back in 1906, when King Alfonso XIII of Spain
was married to Princess Victoria Eugenise of Battenburg. This
wedding, uniting as it did two ancient royal houses, was celebrated
with such pomp and splendour as few are privileged to witness.
Everyone who was anyone was invited to be present. Amongst
those who were invited to this wedding was the Maharaja of
Kapurthala. The wedding was duly celebrated and when it was all
over, the Maharaja went to Seville in Spain to see the famous annual
festival. It was there that he met Anita when she was performing
a dance in a cabaret with castanets, an instrument consisting of
two small shells that clicked together in accompaniment to dance
and music. Nowhere else, the Maharaja was told, were girls of
such beauty and grace to found. That this was no empty boast
was evident when the dancing girls made their appearance, but
the Maharaja was only mildly interested until there appeared on
the floor a girl whose beauty outshone all the others as Venus

outshines the other planets. He was instantly attracted to her and his eyes followed her every movement as she glided over the smooth floor and performed the intricate steps of a sensuous Spanish dance. Her lustrous black hair reflected the gleam of a thousand lights and her sparkling dark eyes shone even brighter. Alone in the middle of the floor, she made a picture only a Zuologa could have paralleled. The Maharaja was infatuated by this enchanting Latin beauty. He sought an interview and within a few days a warm friendship developed between the two. The friendship rapidly grew into love and the Maharaja was not slow in making this known. The girl, strangely attracted to this man, returned his love. He asked her to marry him and she said she would, as soon as her father gave his assent.

So to the father went Anita Delgado and the Maharaja, but instead of offering his blessings, the old man refused to listen to them. He was a seller of hot potatoes on the streets of his native city and the little money he made was not enough to support his family. He depended upon Anita to supplement his income and if she got married his chief support would be taken away from him. No, he would not hear of her marriage.

At last the Maharaja found a solution by presenting the old man with a cheque for $ 6,000. Then there arose other objections. Did not the Maharaja have other wives, the old man asked. Three, he replied, but before he could explain that they would not be at the same level as his beautiful daughter, Anita hastened to assure her father that to her that did not matter. Nothing mattered except her deep love for the Maharaja.

After remaining with her for many years, the Maharaja fell out with her on the suspicion that she was unfaithful to him. The Maharaja and the Maharani were at that time staying at the Savoy Hotel, London. A few staff officers and I were with him at the time. The Maharaja always had two bedrooms, one for himself and the other for the Maharani separated by a drawing room and a passage which opened out to the corridor, but all these rooms formed a part of the Royal Suite reserved for the Maharaja at the Savoy Hotel. After saying 'good night', the Maharaja would retire to his room. On one particular night, the Maharani left her bedroom to meet some friends in the hotel but arranged the bed in such a way that it looked as if she were sleeping with blanket on. The bed was slightly rumpled and the lights were off. A senior attendant of the Maharaja, Khushal Singh who sat in the corridor till the late hours of the night, woke the Maharaja up at 1.30 a.m. and told him that the Maharani had gone to her lover in the same hotel. As the Maharaja was already suspecting her fidelity, he searched her bedroom and found that she was not there. The Maharaja called me and all the other staff officers and we all anxiously awaited the return of the Maharani. She turned up with disheveled hair and in a dressing gown at 3.30 a.m. The Maharaja asked her where she had gone so late in the night. She said that she had gone to her French lady companion as she was not feeling sleepy. The Maharaja said that that was not true. Then she changed her story and, looking at me, said that she was in my room for consultation and advice. The Maharaja again refuted her story and said that he had been to the rooms of all of his officers and not found her there. He told her that she had some illicit love affair with someone in the hotel and therefore he wanted to be separated from her immediately. Khushal Singh, the villain, had already taken the Maharaja to the room of the lady companion and found that she was not there. Khushal Singh also took the Maharaja to several other rooms, including mine, to see whether by any chance she was there. There was an old British Colonel by the name of Enriquez on the staff of the Maharaja who was the tutor and guardian of his grown-up sons. The Maharaja called him and told him that

70

his Maharani had a sexual affair with someone that night. The Maharani fell on the floor and wept bitterly and said that she had not committed any crime nor was she unfaithful to him. The Maharaja did not believe what she said and this terrible and heart-breaking row continued till dawn in my presence. The Maharaja got absolutely worn-out from excitement and retired to his room and asked Colonel Enriquez to prepare the documents of separation immediately.

Mr. M.A. Jinnah, who later became the President of Pakistan, was living in the same hotel. As he and his wife Rita were quite friendly with the Maharaja and the Maharani, they tried to pacify the Maharaja, but he was adamant. Finding that the Maharaja had decided upon separation, they tried to arrange a special maintenance allowance for her. Jinnah sought an interview with the Maharaja and told him bluntly that he could not possibly divorce his wife without any concrete and definite proof of her infidelity. Jinnah by temperament was rude to anyone who confronted him. The conversation between the Maharaja, Jinnah and myself took place in the drawing room of the Maharaja at midday. The Maharaja refused to listen to the advice of Mr. Jinnah who threatened to plead the case of the Maharani with the Secretary of State for India. This interview lasted for an hour. Jinnah was furious and foaming with rage. The Maharaja was still adamant on separation from her and not willing to give her any allowance. Jinnah left in a huff and I followed him. He told me that the Maharaja had no right to discard his wife without any tangible proof of infidelity. A mere report by Khushal Singh and the very fact of her being away for some hours from her bedroom do not legally or morally prove that she had gone to see someone in the same hotel or outside for immoral purposes.

Though all of us, excepting Khushal Singh, persuaded the

Maharaja not to take such a drastic step, the Maharaja did not agree to our pleadings. When I met Jinnah again he was much agitated and annoyed. As a matter of fact, Mr. Jinnah used to ask me to look after his wife Rita when he was away in India, and in fulfillment of my promise to Jinnah, I entertained her in Paris and saw to her comfort in every way during the period of her separation from Mr. Jinnah. He said the Maharaja would have to pay the Maharani *some* alimony for divorcing her.

Prem Kaur started living in a separate bedroom away from the Maharaja's room and negotiations started for an amicable settlement to provide her with a handsome annual allowance for life. Mr. Jinnah succeeded in getting her an allowance of Rs.36,000 a year and an allowance of Rs.24,000 per annum for her son Ajit Singh who was at the time a minor and whom the Maharaja took into his own custody. This was the end of a great romance. The Maharaja suspected her of having sexual relationship with his own son, Maharaja Kumar Mahijit Singh, from the senior Maharani. He threatened to kill himself when the Maharani was so tragically disgraced and his name was associated with her in this scandal.

After the separation, the Maharani lived in a very luxurious and artistically furnished flat in Madrid. She was the proud possessor of gold cutlery and of famous Dresden crockery besides the fabulous jewels that the Maharaja had given her.

14

Prayer Before Passion

Maharaja Jagatjit Singh, after being separated from Prem Kaur, started another love affair with a French lady by the name of Arlette Serry. For several years she stayed with him at his palace in Kapurthala as his mistress. She came to India every winter, to spend a few months with him in his magnificent palace and returned to Paris to join him when he went every year to spend six months of summer and autumn there. She was with him for about six months in a year in Europe and about three months in a year in India. She rented a luxurious apartment in one of the smartest localities in Paris, Avenue Niel near Etoile. The reader will be interested to know that most of the European women with whom the Maharaja of Kapurthala and other Maharajas had love affairs always had two or three more lovers. Mlle. Arlette Serry had a love affair with a journalist, the correspondent of an important newspaper of Buenos-Aires in Paris.

Maharaja Jagatjit Singh of Kapurthala used to pray before the sacred book before he made love to his favourite mistress Arlette Serry on every Friday night. His faithful chief attendant, Sardar Inder Singh, led the prayer. One evening at Pavilion de

Kapurthala, 1 Roué du Champs d'Entrainment, I suddenly came to the prayer room of the Maharaja and found the Maharaja and Inder Singh kneeling before the sacred book. As was normal, I also had to join the prayer and I prayed with them. Afterwards, I enquired from Inder Singh why at this unusual hour at 10 p.m. the Maharaja was praying before the sacred book. He confidentially told me that the prayer was conducted to evoke the blessings of the Almighty to give the Maharaja vigour and strength to satisfactorily perform his sexual duties towards his favourite mistress. After having come to know the purpose of these prayers, I intentionally missed the prayers on Fridays. I also did not inquire, out of sheer discretion, from the Maharaja or from Inder Singh, what the result of the prayer was but I came to know that the Maharaja's prayer was listened to, as the next day he lavishly distributed gifts and presents to his Ministers and staff in cash and kind. I was surprised to get a cheque for 10,000 Francs from the Maharaja without his assigning any reason for this gift, but his attendant told me that the Maharaja was mightily pleased with his performance in bed and that he was lavishly distributing money to his Ministers, Secretary, ADCs and servants, according to their rank, not to speak of Madame Serry who was awarded an emerald necklace from the famous jewellers, Cartier in Rue de La Paix in Paris.

The same thing happened again when I went with the Maharaja to Fezin Moraco and we stayed in Palais Jamal which was once the property and abode of Si Mohamed Ben Ele Arvi El Jamal, Grand Wazir. About this abode of dream and mystery, an Arab poet sang:

O passer-by, stop and think
Admire these beauties and this accomplished marvel
And then say to yourself

74

The mystery is in its inhabitants
And not in the building.

With its mysterious gardens and courtyards, it looked like a dreamland. The garden of the mysterious harem of the powerful Wazir with its beautiful terraces had no parallel anywhere else. The fountains added to the grandeur and beauty of the Palace. The Maharaja occupied the suite of rooms formerly used by the Grand Wazir while Madame occupied the Chamber of the Sultan.

The Maharaja was enamoured of Islamic culture and architecture and was thrilled to hear the early morning Azan prayer from the turrets of the mosques of Faiz. The Maharaja so admired the famous mosque of Marrakesh that he built a similar mosque at Kapurthala, a unique piece of architecture. On one Friday night, the Maharaja was extremely happy with his mistress in this romantic palace and the members of the staff received valuable gifts and increments in their salaries. They always anxiously looked forward to success in his mission so that they could add more gifts to the fortune they had already accumulated. Unfortunately, such a happy event occurred only two or three times a year, and that too, only after the ardent prayers of the Maharaja.

15

Handshake with a Quiver

His Imperial Majesty Haile Selassie, Emperor of Ethiopia, was invited by His Highness Maharaja Jagatjit Singh to a luncheon at his residence at 1 Rue du Champs d' Entrainment in Paris. I was at the time acting as Minister in Waiting to the Maharaja and was asked to arrange his official lunch. His Imperial Majesty came with four noblemen (Rases) who accompanied him to France from Ethiopia, and as soon as the Emperor's car reached the Pavilion de Kapurthala, Sardar Inder Singh, Chief Attendant, wearing gorgeous gold braided uniform and headgear with golden laces, and sporting a huge white beard, went forward to open the door of the Emperor's car. The Emperor and the Rases mistook him for the Maharaja because they had not met him before and offered to shake hands with him. Sardar Inder Singh looked puzzled and did not know what he should do. I was one or two yards away from Inder Singh, in a morning jacket, and I winked at Inder Singh to accept the hand of the Emperor which he did reluctantly. Then the Emperor and the Rases shook hands with me, but as the Rases were tall giants, my hands hurt when they pressed them very hard. Then I loudly said, "Your Imperial Majesty, His Highness the Maharaja is waiting for you at the entrance of the drawing room," in French to avoid any further confusion. So the Emperor and the Rases understood that Inder Singh was not the Maharaja but only an attendant. The Maharaja was dressed in an ordinary lounge suit. I had the honour of meeting the Emperor again when be was in exile after Mussolini's invasion of his kingdom. For my services to him and his kingdom, His Imperial Majesty was pleased to confer upon me one of the highest decorations of his realm, made of solid gold.

The Emperor sits in his medieval throne in his palace in Addis-Ababa with his pet lion Tojo at his side. He is respected by the Muslim Arab world in spite of his being a Christian. Until a few years back, the people had so much respect for the Emperor that they had to crawl on their stomachs when they approached him. Haile Selassie has abolished this custom but still, as in the Home of the Maharajas of India and as in the court of the former Sultans of Turkey, the visitors, must leave his presence backward, in order not to turn their backs on the Emperor.

16

Arlette out of the Net

To continue with her story, Arlette Serry spent two days in the week with the Maharaja in her apartment at Pavilion de Kapurthala, and the remaining days of the week she would sleep in her own flat at Avenue Niel. The Maharaja used to telephone her every evening before dinner and enquire about her welfare. She always replied in the most romantic and sweet language. The Maharaja was mightily pleased every evening after getting such amorous response from his beloved. There was a cook by the name of Anant Khan whom the Maharaja always took to Paris and other places in Europe and America for preparing Indian *pilaws* (fried rice) and dishes for his distinguished guests, and he had a French mistress called Anie who was allowed to stay with him in the servants' quarters at Pavillon de Kapurthala. Anant Khan was always present whenever the Maharaja telephoned Arlette, as the telephone was not very far from the kitchen on the first floor near the dining room. The Maharaja was getting suspicious of Arlette and thought she was having an affair with a journalist and other personal friends as she always preferred to sleep at her own flat rather than at her apartment at the Pavillon.

One night, the Maharaja confided in me that he would like to pay a surprise visit to her at about 9 at night, and he also told Anant Khan to prepare his dinner early so that he could surprise Arlette in her flat. The Maharaja telephoned Arlette and told her that he was very busy entertaining his friends to dinner and wished her 'good night' after exchanging some loving words. Arlette must have heaved a sigh of relief. Then the Maharaja left with me for Arlette's flat. In the meantime, Anant Khan told his French mistress that the Maharaja was on a visit to Arlette. She immediately telephoned to Madame and informed her of the impending visit. The journalist and his friends were dining with her when she got the telephone from the mistress of Anant Khan. With the help of her maidservants and friends, she moved all the plates from the table and after getting rid of the journalists and others, she went to bed pretending to be ill. When the Maharaja arrived he found the flat in darkness and Arlette sleeping soundly. The Maharaja's suspicion was then dispelled. He spent a few hours with her and was quite happy that she was faithful to him.

The Maharaja always gave the title of 'Madame' to all his European mistresses and concubines after the style of the French monarchs Louis XIV, Louis XV and Louis XVI who called their mistresses 'Madame' like Madame de Pompadour and Madame de Maintenor, world famous mistresses of the Kings of France.

Arlette Serry was also carrying on with a Frenchman, Monsieur Pierre Lemont, who was desperately in love with her and made her love him back passionately. She followed his whims and fancies, and one afternoon came in a desperate mood to 1 Rue du Champs d' Entrainment, the residence of the Maharaja, and, with tears in her eyes, told him that she must leave him as she wanted to marry the Frenchman. The Maharaja was much tormented, and informed his courtiers of his pitiable plight. Everyone advised him to leave Paris with her as early as possible and spend some time in another country so that she might forget her lover. It was difficult to persuade Arlette to go with the Maharaja to Berlin when her lover and future husband was watching her movements twenty-four hours of the day and had suspicion that the Maharaja and his staff officers would play some mischief to get rid of him in order to separate him from Arlette. I was deputed by the Maharaja to persuade her to go to Berlin by the next evening's Express train. I went to her flat and pleaded that she could not let the Maharaja go to Berlin without her. At last I was able to prevail upon her to go to Berlin with me. She was not however prepared to go to Berlin the next day with the Maharaja. I fixed the date that suited her to go to Berlin and reserved two sleeping berths for her and for myself. She had kept her impending departure to Berlin a secret, but somehow Mr. X came to know of her plans from her maidservant and rushed to the station with a pistol in his hand to kill me and to bring her back. Luckily, when Mr. X reached the platform, the train whistled and started moving and by the time he could reach the train, it had already moved out of the station.

Arlette was crying the whole night. She was very unhappy that she had left her young lover in the lurch in order to join the Maharaja in Berlin, who had already reached Berlin by the Express train on the fixed date. As soon as Arlette reached Adlon Hotel where the Maharaja was staying, the Maharaja was very pleased that I had succeeded in my mission of bringing her to Berlin. After the Maharaja had dined with her and spent an hour or so in her bed, he allowed her to go and sleep in her own room which was adjacent to his. After some time, finding that the Maharaja had gone to sleep, Madame Serry secretly booked a call to Paris and contacted her lover. He was in a rage and would kill any one for the sake of his love. The next morning, Arlette told me that she must go back to Paris as she was feeling most miserable and could not possibly stay any longer in Berlin. She was torn between two loves, one for the Maharaja because of his money and favours and the other for a man she deeply loved. I advised the Maharaja to let her go, anticipating a lot of trouble from this romantic mad man. I went to see her off at the station when she left for Paris, where she was met at Gare de L'Est by her dashing young Romeo.

17

The Vicereine in a Sari

The Maharajas of the Punjab States, particularly Maharaja Rajinder Singh of Patiala and Maharaja Jagatjit Singh of Kapurthala, were favourites of Lord Curzon of Kedleston, the then Viceroy of India, and also of highly placed British civilians and officers of the Indian Army. They used to go to Simla and mix with British aristocracy and had very intimate and friendly relations with Lady Curzon.

One summer, these two Maharajas were spending their holidays at Simla along with Maharaja Rana of Dholpur. They were lavishly entertaining the Viceroy, the Vicereine, their staff officers and their wives, as well as members of the Viceroy's Council, both British and Indian.

These three Maharajas became more and more friendly with Lady Curzon, and they managed to invite her alone to a dinner at their residence in Simla. Before dinner, they dressed up Lady Curzon in an Indian sari and bedecked her with the historical jewel-studded tiara, pearl necklaces and the famous diamond Eugene, and got her photographed. This photograph, unfortunately for these Maharajas, appeared in the English newspapers to the great anger and wrath of Lord Curzon. He was so much annoyed with Maharaja Rajinder Singh and others for their improper behaviour towards his wife by dressing her in Indian costume with Crown jewels of their States that he passed an order banning not only the visits of these three Maharajas but of all Maharajas of India to Simla without the prior permission of the Viceroy which from then on was normally refused. Maharaja Rajinder Singh took this rebuff to heart and built a summer capital of his own at Chail which is a hill-station about 19 miles from Kandaghat on the way to Simla from Kalka. The hill road to Chail is about 40 miles from Simla. So, instead of going to Sirota, these Maharajas used to have lovely and sumptuous receptions and dinners at Chail, inviting their British friends with their consorts. It is here that a unique cricket ground at the height of about, 7,000 feet was carved out of the hills and cricket matches were played between British, Australian and Indian teams. From the cricket ground, there were splendid views of the Kailas glaciers and the Himalayan summits.

My object in narrating the above story is only to prove how intimate and free were these Maharajas with British men and women and what special affection British women had for them. Otherwise, how was it possible that the wife of the Viceroy of India could dine alone with these three Maharajas?

Even the late Sawai Maharaja Man Singh of Jaipur called Queen Elizabeth, the reigning Queen of England, by her pet name Lizy and spent days and days with her during her visit to Jaipur. Man Singh became the favourite of Elizabeth and was appointed a Staff Officer of the King of England, George VI, father of Elizabeth. His friendship with the Queen created jealousy amongst the Ministers of Rajasthan Government who were given back seats in all receptions organised by the Maharaja in her honour. So much so that Mr. Sukhadia, the then Chief Minister of Rajasthan, complained to Prime Minister Pandit Jawaharlal Nehru about the maltreatment which the Ministers of the Rajasthan Government received at these receptions. The Prime Minister, in his usual exuberance, spoke of the Maharajas of India as an anachronism at a public speech at Ramlila grounds in the presence of the Queen.

18

Love through the Telephone

There are countless weird and untold stories of love affairs between the Maharanis, Princesses and other women of the harems of Indian potentates, and the Ministers and other officials as well as foreigners who, from time to time, visited the States as guests of the rulers.

Here is the true account of a young Indian Princess who was well looked after by her husband but who had no sexual satisfaction from him because of which she had to indulge in many love affairs.

Princess A.D. was the wife of Maharaj Kumar M. Singh, but as the Maharaj Kumar was suffering from cancer, the doctors had advised him not to have any sexual relations with Maharaj Kumari Rani. As he was of a jealous temperament, he was very particular that his wife remained faithful to him and did not go out to another man to satisfy her sexual hunger. The Maharaj Kumari Rani was fond of the Private Secretary to the Maharaja, Sirdar M.D., with whom she often flirted without however having an opportunity for any physical contact. As it was impossible for her to see the Sirdar, she managed to have telephonic conversations with him whenever she was alone in her room. When the telephone talks were later intercepted, and the conversations reported to the Maharaj Kumar, Princess A.D. and Sirdar M.D. refrained from talking to each other on the telephone. Maharaj Kumar M. Singh suspected the weakness of his wife for Sirdar M.D. but he was satisfied that they did not meet each other or communicate with each other.

Under medical advice, the Prince had to go to Paris lor treatment and he took his wife Maharaj Kumari A.D. with him. It so happened that the Maharaja, the father of the Maharaj Kumar, also decided to go to Paris and took Sirdar M.D. with him along with other staff officers. Maharaj Kumar M. Singh and Princess A.D. stayed at the Claridges' Hotel, Avenue des Champs Elysees. The Maharaja and Sirdar M.D. stayed at Hotel George V. The Prince did not allow any contact between the Princess and the Sirdar. However, she had a separate room at the Claridges', fitted with a separate telephone connected to Hotel George V, and so they managed to talk to each other freely and exchanged amorous sentiments, so much so they got into the habit of talking to each other in erotic language every night when the Maharaj Kumar had retired to his bedroom. Both of them got into their beds and as the telephone was placed on a small table near both their beds, they started talking of love in a most passionate manner. As passionate love was an obsession with them, they started talking on the telephone as if they were together in one bed and were making love.

She would describe what sort of pajamas she was wearing and of what colour. The Sirdar, on the other hand, would tell her the colour of his pajamas and whether it was made of silk or ordinary cotton. Then they would say to each other "I kiss you" and "I also kiss you". Then they would say they were undressing. This process continued till they actually forgot that they were only talking to each other on the telephone and that they were not having any physical contact with each other. As in a dream, they felt one with each other and performed all the acts which two lovers would when they make love to each other. This conversation on the love act between them would continue for more than three quarters of an hour when both of them would be sexually aroused. Both the Princess and the Sirdar got full sexual satisfaction in this way and repeated the same every night for five weeks while they were both in Paris. The Maharaj Kumar could never find out that, in spite of the fact that he had fully guarded his wife, she was carrying on her amorous game with her lover though she never had physical contact with him.

As this sort of love affair created mental anguish in both the Sirdar and the Princess, they got tired of this procedure of making love and tried to meet each other and assuage their sexual hunger. This was not possible during the lifetime of the Maharaj Kumar. After his death, the princess and the Sirdar became lovers in the real sense and for many years they were making love to each other though this was resented by the Maharaja.

In order to put an end to this love affair between the Princess and the Sirdar, the Maharaja called the Sirdar and warned him that if he continued to have any amorous relations with the Princess, he would be dismissed. On the other hand, he advised his daughter-in-law to have a Private Secretary of her own who would be given a high salary to be paid from the State Exchequer. The Princess accepted the proposal of the Maharaja, but as the Sirdar was reluctant to give up his post, the Princess appointed Mr. B. Dutt as her private Secretary who, in course of time, became her ardent lover.

Such episodes were common among Maharanis, Princesses and women who had been either educated in foreign countries or brought up in the British society. These women were uncontrollable as they had tasted the life of immorality and passion due to their mingling in European society.

There are many instances of women of the harems of the Maharajas who had lived in European countries and had many escapades. Sometimes a Princess would elope with an Aide-de-Camp of the Maharaja, and if she was unable to leave the Palace with him publicly, she at least was not ashamed of having sexual relations with him to the knowledge of their personal friends.

Out of one hundred emancipated Maharanis and Princesses, my guess is that only 20 were immune to any temptation by the male members of the Palace and not available to the allurements of men. I would like to emphasise that when I am talking of the percentage, I am only mentioning women who had tasted immoral life due to their contacts with men in Europe, America and other parts of the world or even in India at the hill stations.

As emancipated women were free to go to the ballrooms and dance in the arms of passionate men, the physical contact brought about intimacy between them and led them to indulge in sexual pleasures. In ancient times, or even up to the 18th or 19th centuries, a man could not even touch his sister and mother, while in the 20th century men and women dance and clasp each other so closely that in most cases it results in sex indulgence.

Mr. M.N., an I.C.S. officer who was not used to ballroom dancing, once danced with an European woman, and as soon as he held her in his arms and started dancing passionately, he got so excited that he had to stop half-way. Physical contact between a man and a woman, however pure-minded they might be, is likely to produce some sexual excitement between them, and that is why in the sacred books of Hindu philosophy, it is mentioned that men should avoid meeting even their sisters and mothers when they are intoxicated or are not in their senses. But the present civilisation encourages contact between the opposite sexes and this is why the present society, not only in Europe and America but also in Eastern countries, is corrupt and sex-play has become an important part of the life of individuals. Physical contact between the opposite sexes invariably leads to free love and complicates marital life. This process cannot now be checked or controlled as it has already gone out of the control of the human agency. This particularly applies to the younger generation which is revolting against the time-old principles of culture and refinement of the old society. It is a well-known fact that free mixing among young people leads to social promiscuity.

19.

Maharani Indira Raja — the Merry Widow

Princess Indira Raja, the eldest daughter of His Highness Maharaja Rao Gaekwad of Baroda, married His Highness Jatendra Narayan, Maharaja of Cooch Behar. A son and a daughter were born. The daughter was named Gayatri Devi who was later married to Maharaja Sawai Man Singh of Jaipur. The latter was one of the best polo players in the world.

Maharani Indira Raja was the product of Western civilisation and went to Europe and America frequently. After the death of her husband, the Maharani went to England as Maharani Regent during the minority of her son, to look after his studies as he was in an English school. This too was an excuse for going to London very often. Most of the members of the family of Cooch Behar were anglicised. The two sisters of Maharaja Jatendra Narayan, nicknamed Princess Baby and Princess Pretty, were married to two Englishmen who were brothers and spent most of their time in England. Maharani Indira Raja was the idol of British aristocracy. She was fond of alcohol and the gay life a l' Europienne, and I often saw her in a completely hilarious state at private dinner parties in London to which I too was invited by the British aristocracy. To my surprise, one evening I found her sitting on the steps leading to the second floor of the mansion of our host Lord 'X', in the arms of an English friend in an extremely gay and frivolous mood. I sat with them on the steps for a while and then left them alone to join the dinner party.

The Maharani was one of the most attractive, beautiful and elegant women I had ever met, and I was not surprised that she had so many admirers, not only in India but abroad as well. She was also known to be a personal friend of Nawab Kusro Jung of Hyderabad. One afternoon, the Nawab, whom I called Mahboob, telephoned me in Paris that Indira and he were together and I should come and join them in merry-making. I got myself excused on some pretext. Then he gave the telephone to Indira who also spoke to me in the same hilarious tone and invited me to join their fun. Indira and Mahboob seemed to be completely in love with each other and wanted to advertise their love and ventilate their feelings, as it is the natural expression for a passionate love affair. Exhibition of love gives the lovers a quaint mental satisfaction.

After many romantic exploits with Maharanis, the Nawab ultimately got married to a charming woman Miss Lullo Tallyar Khan, scion of a well-known Parsi family, and settled down in Hyderabad. During my last visit to Hyderabad, I met Mahboob and Lullo at their home and was happy to talk to them reminiscently.

20

Maharanis from Abroad

There was a burning desire on the part of the Ruling Princes of India to marry European and American women, particularly Englishwomen. I need not go into the names of all the Maharajas and Princes who married European and American women, but a few instances reveal enough as to how the wind of love was blowing.

His Highness Raja Martanda Tendiman Bahadur Raja of Puthukotta, Ruler of Puthukotta State in south India, got married to an Englishwoman with whom he travelled all over Europe. He gave her many historic jewels of great value as presents. I knew the Raja and Rani of Puthukotta intimately and saw them often at society gatherings in London and Paris and elsewhere. They were very friendly with Maharaja Jagatjit Singh of Kapurthala, who was well-known in European and Parisian society. By virtue of their introduction to the Parisian society by Maharaja Jagatjit Singh, the Tendimans were very cordially received in society.

The Rani was a beautiful, tall woman of elegance, grace and charm. She adapted herself to the Indian way of life and often wore the Indian sari in which she looked like an Indian Maharani.

Another such Maharani was married to his Highness Mahindra Yadvendra Singh Bahadur, Maharaja of Panna, who was first married to the daughter of His Highness the Maharaja of Bhavnagar, and after the death of his first Maharani, married the sister of Maharaja Sawai Man Singh of Jaipur. He too was fond of travelling in the company of British women, leaving the Maharani at hill-stations during summer vacations, to enjoy herself to her heart's content. The Maharani of Panna gave brilliant receptions to which she invited British officers and their wives and the elite of Mussoorie, including Princes and Princesses of Royal blood and young Indian officers who indulged in the usual merry-making and flirtations and love tangles in her beautiful and artistically furnished house. I had the pleasure of visiting her often and partaking of the lavish hospitality of the Maharani who was most alluring and sexy in her looks.

Another Begum was the wife of His Highness Nawab Sir Taley Mohammed Khan, Nawab of Palampur. She was of British descent. The Nawab bedecked her with historical jewels and she travelled with him all over Europe. The family of the Nawab was of Afghan origin belonging to the Yusufa Honi tribe. Following the footsteps of his father, the son also married an Englishwoman.

Raja Natwar Singhji of Porbunder in Gujarat State was married to Princess Rupali, the daughter of Daulat Singhji of Limbdi. He had no issue from her and she died. At present, Natwar Singhji is living with an Englishwoman at Ootacamand in Mysore State. He maintains her by selling his jewels.

After the integration of the States with India, this ruler seldom visited his former State, and if he ever does so now, he goes there only to sell his jewels and furniture. Even the houses and palaces given to the ex-rulers have been sold and the money realized by the sale of these properties deposited in foreign banks, particularly in Switzerland where, under Swiss law, strict secrecy about the name of the depositor is kept.

Maharaja Tukoji Rao Holkar of Indore, and his son who succeeded him, were married to American women. Maharaja Ranbir Singh Rajinder Bahadur, Ruler of Jind State in the Punjab, who was stone deaf, was married to an Englishwoman called Dorothy.

21

Sensationally Vindictive Princesses

It would be of interest to the readers to know how some of the Maharanis, when caught in the tight grip of passion, used to quench their anger and take vengeance by resorting to all sots of unheard of cruelties.

The Begum of Junagadh was seen by her young maid-servant, Shamim, making love to her lady companion as both of them were lesbians. Shamim told the story to the servants and the whole palace staff knew that the Begum was carrying on love affairs with her lady companions. In order to punish her for her impudence and insolence and to teach her a lesson, the Begum got the other servants to beat her and have her legs, feet and hands tied. Then she put red pepper and acid into her vagina with her own hands. Shamim cried out in pain but no soothing ointment or medicine was applied to her burnt parts, and after struggling desperately for life, she died. The Begum tried to hush the matter up, but the other servants raised a hue and cry and the matter was reported to the police by the advocate engaged by the parents of the dead girl and the case was registered at the police station. The case was fought in the Lahore High

Court, where, by the intervention of the Pakistan authorities it was withdrawn to save the bonour of the Begum.

His Highness Tikko Rao Pawar, Maharaja of Dewas State, was married to the daughter of the Maharaja of Kolhapur, Her Highness Akka Sahib. She was a very authoritative and arrogant woman and always dominated her husband. Owing to the strained relationship between them, the Maharani started regular campaigns involving Maharaja Tikko Rao in political difficulties. In the end, with the help of the political department of the Government of India, she succeeded in putting the Maharaja in a tight corner. The Maharaja should either abdicate or accept a commission of enquiry. The allegations against the Maharaja were that he was misruling the State and that he had created Jagirs in favour of his daughters begotten of the second wife whom the Government of India did not recognise as a regular consort of his. The Maharaja did not accept the conditions of the Government of India and fled to Pondicherry where be lived for three years as Ruler of Dewas State with a council of regency ruling on his behalf in the State. He was well-protected by the Governor of Pondicherry which was then a colony of the French Government.

The trouble between the Maharaja and the Maharani mainly arose as the Maharaja fell in love with the maidservant of the Maharani. He brought her from Kolhapur in his royal railway saloon to Dewas and kept her at the palace, first as a mistress and later as his morganatic wife.

The Maharani was so vindictive that she started living in Kolhapur and left Dewas for ever, but her haughty temperament found its display even in Kolhapur where she became very unpopular. She used to go twice a week to the Mahalakshmi Temple on foot and ordered that no citizen should be walking on that road at the time she was going to the Temple. If by

H H Jagatjit Singh in Turkey

H H Jagatjit Singh with P.M. Ramsay MacDonald, London

Jarmani Dass in London

H H Jagatjit Singh with foreign visitors

H H Jagatjit Singh with H H Maharaja of Mysore
with his Cricket Team

H Ḣ Jagatjit Singh in the Far East

H H Jagatjit Singh in Hollywood

H H Jagatjit Singh dancing with a foreign lady

A Princess of the royal family

A member of the royal family

Mme De Maria with Jarmani Dass in Paris

Miss Germaine Pallgrino

One of the foreign visitors to Punjab

Parvathi Devi

Sita Devi

Rani Anari Devi

Rani Kanari of Kangra

H H Jagatjit Singh and his family

Laila with H H Yuvraj of Mysore and Jarmani Dass

Anita Delgado with Jarmani Dass

chance a man or a woman was seen loitering about in her way, she would take a whip and strike the person.

There are many more instances where Maharanis were most vindictive, but I need not dwell upon them any more. Behind the scenes, there were murders and assassinations by the Maharajas when they caught the Maharanis at their game. The Maharajas were extremely jealous of their Maharanis, and if they had any illicit connection with any man without their approval or permission, they had to undergo heavy punishment. There were cells in the prisons for such convicted Maharanis and the Maharaja's decision was the last word in law. There was no appeal against his orders. There were many instances when the Maharajas shot the lovers of their Maharanis with their own hands and then attended their cremation ceremonies as if their death was due to natural circumstances. Many Maharajas killed the husbands of the women they wanted to make them their Maharanis. This was done with the connivance of the British Government whose policy was to win over the Rulers of India by means fair or foul.

Normally, aged rulers married young Maharanis and allowed their younger relatives and young members of their staff to mix with them. In most cases, it resulted in love affairs between the Maharanis and the young men. Maharanis of mature age were satisfied with physical relations with old Saints and Sadhus who had free access to them. In the case of the Begums, the Syeds had a glorious time with them, to my personal knowledge.

22

British Policy and Indian Potentates

Due to the taste which men in the upper strata of society
acquired for European women, there were frequent marriages
with them. Those who could not marry them due to personal
or domestic reasons took them as their mistresses. They lived
with them publicly in England and the continents of Europe
and America. Some even brought them over to India and lived
with them in the palaces in total disregard of their legitimate
consorts. Many Maharajas and Princes bought houses, chateaus
and villas in England, France and other places, where they spent
their summer vacations with their European wives or mistresses,
and entertained them their friends lavishly at their residences.
Everywhere in the big hotels in London, Paris, Berlin, New York
and other capitals of the world, huge receptions and dinner
parties were arranged by these Maharajas and Princes and these
were attended by their European or American mistresses and
the cream of the society of world capitals. Sexual and illicit
connections between the Indians, Europeans and Americans
were encouraged and were more numerous during 1910-1940.
After India obtained independence in 1947, marriages between
Indians and Europeans and Americans declined.

As long as Lord Curzon of Kedleston remained the Viceroy of India (till 1902), his dynamism and powerful personality were felt by all who came in contact with him. He had in his time discouraged marriages between Indian Rulers and Europeans, and gone to the extent of passing orders and enacting a law that no issue of an Indian Ruler from his European wife would be considered as successor to the throne of his father. Though Lord Curzon believed in the supremacy of the British ways of Western civilization, yet he advocated gradual elevation of the Indians to the level of the British in cultural progress. Curzon felt that the microscopic minority of Englishmen could not exist in India for a long time amidst hundreds of millions of Indian people. Curzon was appointed Viceroy of India in 1898, when he was barely 39 years old.

At that time, the tendency of the Ruling Princes and their sons was to marry European and American women, and had Lord Curzon not passed such an act of succession, most among the Princely Order would have married European women and in due course of succession, the whole of the territory of Indian States would have passed into the hands of the descendants of European and American women. This law was a great curb on the Rulers of Indian States. The European women also found that they were not gainers in marrying Indian potentates and preferred to remain as their mistresses with dignified titles bestowed upon them by the Maharajas which were recognised by the then Government of India. During this period, the Indian Rulers were even reluctant to go to Europe for merry-making as Lord Curzon impressed upon them a sense of duty towards their States.

The object of my writing about the Maharajas, their marriages and their love affairs with British women and of the amorous illicit connections of the Maharanis with the British and Indian officers — Civil and Military — is to show how, from 1910 onwards to 1940, it was the game of the British Government to entice the former Rulers of the Indian States and their Ministers into serious love affairs with British women for two purposes. Firstly, it was to get hold of the wealth of the rulers and, secondly, to gain political power. The British in India and England were most friendly with the rulers of the Indian States, their Ministers and members of their staff. They mingled with them on equal terms and had no hesitation in encouraging their women to have intimate relations with them.

The way of life of these rulers when they were abroad, particularly in England, with whom India was in constant touch in all fields — political, economic, cultural, social and educational — was quite different from the way of life led by them in India.

In England, the Queens were well-known for their love affairs. Queen Elizabeth, daughter of King Henry VIII and Anne Boleyn, had many lovers amongst the courtiers. She lived a life of magnificence and feasting and occupied a great deal of her time in balls, banquets and similar other amusements. The life of refined luxury led by the Queens of France and other countries of Europe, as associated with Empress Josephine, Empress Marie Louise and Empress Marie Antoinette in the time of Napoleon Bonaparte and Louis XVI of France, respectively, is well-known. At that time it was not considered improper in French society that the Kings and Emperors could have as many mistresses as they wished to. The frivolity of sex and love of these great Queens and monarchs make the pages of the history of France colourful in the 18th and 19th centuries. The love exploits of Josephine and other Queens of Europe are narrated in another chapter of this book.

From time immemorial, Indian queens like Sita, Draupadi,

Rani of Jhansi, Nurjahan and Mumtaz Mahal, have been revered. Mata Sundri and Mata Gujri were the noble and heroic consorts of the great Gurus of the Sikh religion. No historian could find any flaw in the character of these great queens, but with the advent of British power in India, the character of Indian women underwent a complete change, particularly in the ruling houses of India. The rural areas of India were not so affected by the influence of the British and the standard of morality of Indian women in the villages remained the highest in the world.

In the beginning, when the British came to India, they refrained from meeting the Indians. But, after the proclamation of Queen Victoria as Empress in 1857, and even much earlier, British officers were posted all over the country in every nook and corner. When businessmen and traders and tea planters made their headquarters in different parts of India, particularly in south India and East Bengal, they married Indian women and started mixing with Indians. They created a community called Anglo-Indians which is an important minority in India today.

Englishmen started keeping Indian women from the poor and lower classes of the Indian population as concubines, particularly in Kerala and East Bengal, and many Englishmen even married them.

In America when a white American marries a Red Indian or a coloured woman, the offspring is classified as half-American, one-third American, one-fourth American, one-sixth American, one-sixteenth American and one-twentieth American. This means that in the chain of marriages, the blood and colour of the offspring change. In several generations, the blood becomes closer and closer to the white man or the other way about. But this system was not known in India.

It is interesting to mention here that in some of the Christian families of Kerala, half the members are of dark complexion while the other half are fair. I enquired of my personal friends from Kerala how they could explain this vast difference in complexion. They explained to me that, if one brother marries a girl of white complexion, his children will be fair, while if his brother marries a dark girl, his children will be dark. And if the process is repeated through several generations, the colour of the descendants turns black and white in accordance with the colour of the forefathers and mothers.

As I mentioned before, the Maharajas of India went to England and France and other parts of the world with their British and European mistresses and neglected their own Maharanis and concubines. Therefore, the women could not but fall a prey to the lure of British officers and Indian Don Juans. This was the main case of the happenings at Mussoorie, Simla, Dalhousie, Darjeeling, Mount Abu, Ootacamund and other hill resorts which were well-known for merry-making and frivolity. The women of the higher strata of society and the Maharanis and Ranis also attended big races in cities like Bombay, Calcutta and Madras, and even owned horses and played for high stakes. There was no check on them to control their finances and their passion for gambling and sex, as they had a lot of money and resources at their disposal and the Maharajas were away in foreign countries. It was in this period that the Maharanis, Princesses and even other Indian women with Western education in the high strata of society began to find greater pleasure in the company of Britishers and Indian lovers than in that of their own husbands. The Maharajas spent the greater part of the year in foreign countries and, on return, brought with them their foreign mistresses, lodged them in their palaces, and forced the Maharanis to accept them as their equals. Therefore, there was bitter discontent among the Maharanis and other palace women.

23

Eunuchs as Guardians of Chastity

It is interesting to know how Emperors, Turkish Sultans, the Nizams of Hyderabad and the fabulous Maharajas of India were able to control their large harems, some times numbering 300 to 500 women. There was a regular system of control for these women.

The women were trained and brainwashed to live only with one man. To check them from falling into the hands of other men, a number of devices were used. Firstly, it was impossible for any woman to get out of the chain of barriers spread all around her. There were, at the time of the Turkish Sultans, eunuchs to guard the harems and the Chief Eunuch had the title of His Highness and the office of Grand Chamberlain. He ranked just below the Prime Minister and above all the other Ministers of the Government. He was the custodian of the harem and his word was law. He had under his command a big regiment of women guards surrounding the harems, well-armed with pistols and guns.

Then there was a strong system of spying. Any woman going astray was reported by the Woman Officer of the Guard to His

Highness the Grand Eunuch. Punishment was very severe and heavy. Sometimes death sentences were imposed. There was great fear and awe in the minds of the women of the harem. All the same, there were quite a few cases of infidelity.

Similar was the case in the palaces of the Indian Kings. They had a very intricate system of checking the movements of their Maharanis and Ranis. During the several years of my stay in the Court of Patiala where I was intimately connected with the Maharani, I did not come across a single instance of any Maharani or Rani going astray. It was beyond the comprehension of any woman to mix with any other man except her husband.

The Great Mughals and Sultans of Turkey put further checks on the women by specifying a certain conduct for living, and only a certain kind of food was supplied to them which would not make them excessively passionate. Even boys of five years and above were not allowed in the harems of Mughal Emperors and the Sultans of Turkey. Even the nearest male relations were not admitted to visit their women relations in the harems, except on special occasions such as marriages and deaths, and that too with permission.

It is very interesting to depict here the inner apartments of a palace which would show how the women were isolated from the outside world. To reach the inner apartment, six or seven corridors had to be traversed. The inner apartment of Maharani Kaushallya was heavily guarded by old men and women. Further away, the corridors were well guarded by eunuchs and deformed hunchback dwarfs. These persons were specifically detained for such duties because of their detachment from life and their impotence in sex. It was meant to guard the chastity and purity to which great importance was attached by the society described in the epics.

24

Indian society and Pseudo-modernity

Recently, I attended a dinner party at the magnificent house of a friend of mine in New Delhi to which he and his wife had invited many important personalities, including industrialists, business magnates, politicians, Secretaries to the Government of India and their wives, and two Maharanis. Two ladies in this party, after a few drinks, told me with a twinkle in their eye that they were shortly going to Paris for a holiday. When I asked them whether they were going alone or with their husbands, they again twinkled their eye, expressing gleefully that they were going alone. They asked me whether I would be going there alone and whether I could get them invited to Paris by the French Government in my capacity as President of the Indo-French Friendship Association. I told them that whether I was there or not, when they get there they would be well-looked-after by my foreign friends in Paris. From their talk I understood that these beautiful ladies preferred to go alone without their husbands to have complete freedom as well as to enjoy life according to their whims and fancies.

It was not the first time that I had such a conversation at a dinner party. Usually, I find that women of high society feel happier in going abroad without their husbands. In many cases, it is a pre-arranged affair and their male friends meet them in Paris, London, Frankfurt and other capitals of Europe. Sometimes they go alone as far as Canada and U.S.A. and after a few days of stay in these countries, they come to Paris and other capitals of Europe to meet their beloveds and spend some time with them before returning to India separately. I know some prominent women of Delhi who went to Paris alone and were met by their lovers, and thereafter they returned from U.S.A. where they had gone on an official errand. By this arrangement, no suspicion about their meeting was created and the identity of the lovers remained undisclosed. Some time ago, Mr. Z, one of the highest and most distinguished personalities of India, went to U.S.A. on an official tour and asked Mr. and Mrs. A to meet him in Paris from where he picked them up and took them to U.S.A. as members of his family and dropped them back to Paris from where they returned alone. Their air fares to U.S.A. and back to Paris and board and lodging in Paris and U.S.A. were paid by the host of Mr. Z.. Mr. A had connived at the love affair between his wife and Mr. Z who was authorised to take with him a couple of his relatives at Government expense without infringing Government rules or conventions. However, everything is fair in love and war.

It is a common practice that officers going on tour with female officers spend many days in rest houses and hotels together where they develop a deep friendship, often ending in love affairs. In almost all cases, constant companionship between men and women induces them to have a sexual relationship. There are many cases where an unmarried female officer found a suitable husband during her official tour. I know many instances where female I.A.S. officers married I.A.S. men by coming in contact with them during their official tours, but often love is developed between married men and married women during these official tours to the catastrophic unhappiness of both. Many such cases are there to my knowledge.

Further, some Government officials take their female stenographers and female secretaries with them on official tours and stay together in hotels and rest houses. Sometimes the officers take them in their cars for a drive on the pretext of dictating important and secret letters, but in reality they mean to have an opportunity to play with the women. As the Chairman of a Medical Institution, I attended a Board meeting in Delhi for the selection of candidates for appointments. The doctor in charge had advertised in the newspapers that there were vacancies in the hospital and the candidates should send their photographs along with their applications. The doctor asked the female candidates many questions regarding their qualifications to find out whether they were suitable for the post. He also asked them individually whether they would be prepared to go out on tours with him alone. Most of the women who were in dire need of employment, replied affirmatively, and the others said that they would have to consult their parents. Naturally, the Doctor rejected the application of the latter then and there since they did not fit in with his plans. Out of 50 candidates he selected only 10, who according to him were eligible as they were prepared to go on tours with him alone and were young and beautiful and ready to flirt with him. I asked the doctor whether it was proper for him to put such questions to the candidates. The Doctor said it was an essential question as he had to go on tours very often to Chandigarh, Patiala, Ghaziabad, etc., and particularly to Mussoorie hill-station, where he had a clinic and required assistants with him for giving injections to the patients. Later on, I came to know what he was up to. There were serious complaints about his conduct as reported to me by the staff of the institution. So I told the Doctor that I would not remain as Chairman of the Board of Directors as he had misused his position to molest these women. The Doctor apologised to me and said that in future he would refrain from his amorous activities.

Most of the star hotels in Delhi have call-girls. These call-girls work in collaboration with the reception officers of the hotels who introduce them to the tourists. The girl and the reception officers are well-paid. Luxurious suites of the five-star hotels are reserved for callgirls who come from Calcutta, Bombay and other places by aeroplanes. The bills of the hotels are paid by rich businessmen who want to have a contract or a license from Government officials who by the allurements of trained courtesans, accede to their request. Some hotels have engaged beautiful and young female sweepers and room-maids to attract the tourists and entertain them.

Recently, I was invited to drinks by a German friend at a five-star hotel. Within a few minutes of my arrival, a good-looking girl of about 20 with a comely body entered the room and began dusting. My friend knew her well and asked her to sit down.

In the high strata of society, I include women belonging to the aristocracy, the Princely Order, business and industrial magnates, Secretaries to the Government, high civil and military officials and the upper middle class. I do not depict here the life of Indian women in the lower strata of society or the life of those living in the villages where modem civilization and culture, as imported from the West, have not so far affected morals and character. However, life in the villages is changing rapidly with the advent of the cinema, radio and modem education, on account of which the villagers are in a position to read novels and sexy literature in the vernacular languages. There is undoubtedly a great influx of modem ideas into the villages and serious infiltration of modem European thought. It will not be a matter of great surprise if, in long years, the villagers adopt the same modernised culture as adopted in the urban areas, forgetting their own traditional culture and virtues.

Let us for a moment picture to ourselves the present state of mind of women in the high circles, particularly those who are Western in their outlook and have received Western education in schools and colleges. As most of them were educated in the Christian mission schools and Westernised institutions in India where Indian culture or religious teachings are not encouraged, gradually the present generation is shifted from their traditional values. By constant aloofness from their own culture and religion and by imitating the culture of other faiths, they are neither here nor there. As Western culture taught them to pursue and gain material prosperity in life more than spiritual or moral well-being, they are all the time actively engaged in the pursuit of high positions, luxurious houses and furniture, cars and all the Western equipments such as frigidaires, air-conditioners, radiograms, electric cookers and electric washing machines. So much so that women in elite society feel ashamed of following the rituals of their own religion and openly declare that they do not believe in the old practices and sacred rituals of their religion. The result is that they are in a perpetual state of confusion and mental disorder. We should not follow the decadent society of the West. The so-called emancipation of such Westernised Indian women is in reality a degradation.

Further, due to economic factors, the luxurious way of living under modem conditions, and the cultural influence of the West, Indian society has undergone a big change and women with primary and secondary standards of education prefer to work in offices, while those who are highly educated go in for I.A.S. and other Indian services, where they are constantly in the company of male colleagues and develop deep friendships with them. Now you find that about 25 per cent of the staff working in the offices of the Government of India and the State Governments are women. The total number of posts in Government departments runs into millions and as 25 per cent of these posts are being filled by women, their number also runs into hundreds of thousands. It is unfortunate that women who had formerly no occasion to mix with men due to the social conditions prevailing in the country, suddenly find themselves face to face with men in the offices and sit side by side with their male colleagues. As nature would have it, the majority of these women make friends with men, which very often leads to serious love affairs. In the past, women were not allowed by their parents or husbands to invite male friends to their houses and only personal friends of their husbands were allowed to meet them, but the service girls meet the boys in their offices and go out with them and mix with them intimately, and also invite them to their homes. Many service girls have private flats where they receive their boy friends in intimacy. So, the old view that women should not be free with men is no longer accepted by modern women. Again, due to the freedom enjoyed by women there are mishaps, and women become pregnant, and as the law forbids abortion, they go in for abortion by secret means and there are many cases of deaths in the process.

The other day I read in the newspaper that a woman was slapped by her husband on the very first night of their marriage as he found her not to be a virgin. A well-known writer condemned the action of her husband who forgot that 60 to 70 per cent of the modern girls were not virgins, particularly those in the universities as students, nurses in the hospitals, clerks in the offices of the Government departments and private firms and others earning their livelihood as working girls, and those belonging to the high strata of society and the upper middle class. It is interesting that the Italian Supreme Court is seized of the question whether it is a crime for a girl to pretend that she is a virgin.

Not long ago a man in Naples agreed to marry his fiancée on condition that she was a virgin and the fiancée asserted that she was a virgin, but in fact it turned out to be false. Her husband went to his lawyer on the morning after the first wedding night and applied for legal separation on the ground that his wife had caused him grave mental and physical suffering. The case went on for five years until at last the High Court agreed that the wilful lie constituted a criminal offence. The husband was granted legal separation.

In olden times, on the first night of a married couple, the family members sat outside the nuptial bedroom. When it was declared by the husband that the woman was a virgin, there was rejoicing among them. A large piece of cloth was kept on the nuptial bed. After the performance of the marital rites, the husband brought it outside to show to his parents and relatives to be soaked in blood. Then there was great ovation and the bride was honoured. In the present society, no husband dares to ask his young wife on their first night to give proof of her virginity. Some husbands, out of simple shame or excessive courtesy or unwillingness to injure the feelings of their lifelong partners, keep quiet and accept their brides to be virgins even if in reality they are not. Then, some women play tricks on their husbands. They keep red ink under their pillows and sprinkle it on the white sheet and thus gain the confidence of their husbands. Then again, according to medical theory, after a certain age the membrane of virginity on the uterus gets dissolved by itself. I do not want to generalise this statement as there are still women who have full control over their passion and would not surrender to the advances of men under any circumstances.

What has further demoralised the society in India is the lewdness of shows in hotels and restaurants. So much so that some restaurants in Bombay have cabaret shows with breakfast consisting of tea and coffee and Chinese omelette at Rs.85 per person and it is served from 6.30 a.m. to 8 a.m. Those who are fond of cabarets visit these restaurants even as early as 6.30 a.m.. In Delhi, some of the restaurants have cabarets by practically naked dancing and singing girls with only a black string to cover the vaginal parts to evade the strict nudity laws of the country. Strip-tease shows in India generally end in a vulgar way, while the strip-tease show at the world famous Crazy Horse Restaurant in Paris is a most artistic masterpiece. The cabaret girls at the Crazy Horse are most beautiful with slim and shapely figures. In a small restaurant in which the capacity of accommodating the clients is limited, small stools are brought and the clients flock in like a herd of sheep. It is the most elegant gathering rubbing shoulders with the most beautiful Parisiennes intoxicated with champagne and other alcoholic drinks. The show girls are not allowed to mix with the customers, nor can they come and sit at the tables and drink with them as they can in some of the restaurants in Delhi, Bombay and Calcutta. It is art for art's sake and not vulgarity.

25

Gala Gaiety in Big Cities

Now I come to society life in the big cities of India. The advent of ballroom dancing, strong alcoholic drinks and body friction between the opposite sexes while dancing closely leave little chance for the women to resist. I attended some dinner parties where some women went for dancing with pre-arranged lovers and returned to the table long after the band had ceased to play. Some society women even went away to some hotels with their lovers, leaving their husbands in the party to dance with other guests. So it takes place in some clubs and five-star hotels of Delhi. I watched dozens of such instances this year not only in Delhi but also in Calcutta and Bombay. No question is asked by their husbands or relatives as to why they stayed for so long with their dancing partners after the dance was over. In the offices, many senior officers carry on with their female secretaries, stenographers and clerks. In one or two offices, I noticed that a board was hung and red light switched on to indicate that the officer was busy and should not be disturbed. Some personal friends confided in me that the board was hung outside the office to indicate that they were busy with their official work and were dictating important and secret notes and letters to their female stenographers without any disturbance, while actually they were busy flirting with them without creating any suspicion in the minds of their subordinate officers. The peon sitting outside is in the know of what is happening inside and he is highly tipped to keep his mouth shut.

Many officers sit in the office till late at night, pretending that they were busy with the files in the office though they were busy in having amorous relations with their lady stenographers and assistants.

Some women live with Sadhus and Babas in the guise of religion, since the Sadhus are not suspected of having any desire for sexual relationship with women. I have got numerous examples of Sadhus having sexual relationship with their female disciples. It is true that in the Epic and Vedic times, some of the great saints were allowed to cohabit with Maharanis and Princesses who had no issue in order to create sacred and pure blood in the dynasties. But that was done with the knowledge and acquiescence of their husbands and the permission of religion which recognised and sanctioned the moral code of society. Today the women go for passion even with the saintly order of the Sadhus and have sex orgies. I can go on quoting examples to show that the trend of women today is towards sex and sex alone and that India will not be following the traditional values of her great culture but will fall into the cesspool of moral degradation as is happening in some of the Western countries.

26

Women's Values — Old and New

Due to various circumstances, especially the lack of religious influence on the minds, women take pride in selecting a life which is glamorous and pleasant but in reality is aimless, unsatisfying and vulgar. Even in the tribal communities like the Red Indians, there are women who have got a high sense of morality and they stick to one man all their life. When I went to Chicago, I met some Red Indian women and they told me that they believed in this principle. On a photograph which I got from a Red Indian princess, she wrote "true to one man".

In modern India, it is not possible to segregate the sexes. So it is important to give sex education to women and make them aware of the evils of sex orgies. If women of India start believing in the traditional values that their happiness or unhappiness depends on the life they lead, they are bound to feel happy and at peace. And not go astray.

To make a home happy, the first principle should be love for the home. There should be division of work between man and woman. The man should work to earn the livelihood for the members of his family. The woman should look after the

115

house and children and make it a paradise. With this division of work the home would become happy and India will become prosperous and great.

Some women advertise in the newspapers for matrimonial alliances, but in reality it is a ruse to find someone who could be a lover. What a vulgarity it is when the parents advertise in the newspapers for suitable matches for their daughters in the same way as for selling cars.

Recently, there has been a big controversy in the country started by the former Chief Minister of U.P. that women should not be given responsible positions in life. He has stated that in administration, they were found to be unfit. Women challenged his statements and gave an account of the heroic episodes connected with the women of India. I personally do not agree with what the Chief Minister has said, namely, that women are unfit to hold high positions in the I.A.S. and I.F.S. and in the Army, Navy and Air Forces. I am of the opinion that women are capable of holding any position in the country, and this has been proved by the elevation of Mrs. Indira Gandhi to the high office of Prime Minister of India, Mrs. Bandaranaike as Prime Minister of Ceylon and of Mrs. Golda Meir as Prime Minister of Israel.

But I take another view altogether. I feel that women can play a more important and useful part at home than in politics, services, or administration. What a great sense of honour and pride there is for women to look after husband and children and enjoy their family life instead of working in offices, and coming back dead tired in the evening. The result is that they have no time to get good food prepared for the family members and look after the home and children. The husband and wife do not have enough time to have intimate talks with each other on family matters and to spend a few hours of bliss which it

116

is the duty of the wife to provide for the husband who comes home tired after a hard day's work. Due to lack of proper social intercourse, sex remains in a dormant state. It is essential for sexual pleasure that the husband and wife eat together and talk about intimate matters and feel in complete harmony with each other.

There is a serious movement in America for equality of status for men and women, but there is also a movement against it. Here in India, women have begun to feel that they have an inferior status to men. Laws have been enacted against the Vedic principles of marriage. The Constitution of India has provided for the equality of man and woman, and on no account can any woman be debarred from occupying the highest post, i.e., the President of India, but still the women are not satisfied. They want more and more power to subdue men. Women in the services, and particularly in high posts, dominate their husbands, with the result that mutual love or confidence between them is gone. In the upper classes, wives are becoming nagging monsters and behave like superior beings. They do not inspire love and respect in the family. Take the case of any animal. The female is docile and surrenders to the male while the male is aggressive and good. Swami Vivekanand said, after returning from America, that women in India looked feminine and attractive, but unfortunately today women in India are taking the place of American women. They wear chiffon and high coiffeurs, and their mouths are reddened with lipstick, and the eyebrows blackened, the black lines above the eyebrows giving them the look of a professional prostitute.

Unfortunately, under our secular Government, religious education is not given in schools and colleges, and so it is natural that the children coming out of these schools and colleges have no idea of our traditional values, of our ancient philosophy and culture. So they are apt to become materialistic in every sense of the word. This is the root cause of the mental confusion among the young members of the nation. They feel that religious education in public institutions is not necessary. People practise religion for getting peace of mind and are able to mould their character in such a way as to have peace of mind and prove to be good citizens, in every respect. If they do not want to practise any religion let them go for an idol of their own imagination and worship it. There should be some fear of the Superior Power to control the minds of different people in the world. In a secular State, individuals with no fear of the Superior Power and no fear of being condemned by their community, are apt to go astray. This is why, in a secular State, discipline no longer exists. Secular society continues to be the amalgam of all religions, and future generations will be further away from the control which society exercises over their minds. The present society is more for material progress than for achieving spiritual upliftment by following a religion. The sole motive in life is to make money, by illegal and dishonest means if necessary. This is why women have developed an unimaginably different outlook on life and work all the time for enhancing their material and economic advancement and for getting satisfaction in day-to-day life with excitement and sex.

Women are spending more money on luxuries now and they consider it their legitimate right to do so. The culture of the modern woman is in how much money and jewellery she possesses, how luxuriously her house is run and what beautiful furniture there is in her house. It is this culture of theirs which is apparent to the outside world which encounters them. The former idea of spending money on pilgrimage and on charity and giving alms to the poor has vanished from the minds of modern women. They hardly realise that the way of life that they are leading is neither good for the country nor for themselves. They have a horror of going back and imitating the life led by their mothers and grandmothers. I am not personally against Western education, but our traditional values of life and our ancient culture should not be forgotten. It is true that the Hindu religion is a muddle and is not comprehensible to most of the modern educated young men and women. It is, therefore, in the interest of the Hindus to make their religion as simple as possible and as comprehensible as it can be done with the help of sages, teachers and savants. They must reduce the huge volume of Vedas, Puranas and sacred books into a consolidated text where one could find solace and peace of mind. There is a well-known saying: "What a happiness it is to be able to dispense with the company of people one does not care for. Therefore, it is essential to move in the society of people whom one cares for."

27

Sita — Queen of Virtue

If we desire to see the model of unbounded devotion, resignation and love, let us look at the picture of Sita, as presented by Valmiki, the Milton of the Golden Age. Nothing more beautiful or sentimental can be culled even from *Paradise Lost*. Rama was about to abandon his faithful wife for the purpose of becoming a *vanaprasthi* or hermit when she thus poured out her ardent love, pleading to share his exile:

"A woman's bliss, Oh Lord! is found not in the smile of a father, mother, friend, nor in herself.

Her husband is her only partner here,

Her heaven hereafter.

If thou indeed depart this day into the forest drear, I will precede and smooth the thorny way... a gay recluse.

On thee attending, happy shall I feel within the honey-scented grove to roam,

For thou, even here canst nourish and protect and therefore other friend I cannot need.

And thus resolved, I may not be denied.

Rest and wild fruit shall be my constant food;
Nor do I mean to add unto thy cares,
Nor lag behind, nor forest food refuse,
But fearless traverse every hill and dale....
Thus could I sweetly pass a thousand years;
But without thee e'en heaven would lose its charm.

. . . .

Happily embracing thy feet I shall reside
In the rough forest as in my father's house.
Void of all other wishes supremely thine,
Permit me this request — I will not grieve
I will not burden thee — refuse me not, O Lord
But shouldst thou Raghuvar, this prayer deny —
Know, I resolve on death."

28

Nurjahan — Queen of the Rose Scent

One of the striking personalities of the Mughal period was Empress Nurjahan, daughter of Itimad-ud-Daula. She was married to Jahangir in 1611 A.D. She was a courageous woman and was endowed with the capacity of undertaking affairs of the State and taking active interest in matters of administration. She cajoled the unwilling, helped the needy, strengthened the wavering, made firm promises, and gave faith to all.

Nurjahan would sit in the balcony of her palace while the nobles presented themselves listening to her dictates. Coins were stuck in her name with the caption "By order of King Jahangir — Gold has a hundred splendours added to it by receiving the impression of the name of Nurjahan the Begum." In all *'firmans'* receiving the Imperial signature, the name of Queen Nurjahan Begum was jointly attached. Coins were struck in her name and the Royal seal bore her signature. The noblemen had to dismount from their horses when they saw her. They could not see her personally. Messages were sent through the eunuchs employed for this purpose.

Ikbul, the Rajput wife of Mughal Emperor Jahangir and

mother of Prince Khusru, was also given the title of Shah Begum by the Emperor.

Here is the story of Nurjahan and Emperor Jahangir which is a most telling depiction of a true picture of the character and the fidelity of the women of the period extending from the 12th century to the 17th century. Among the lower strata of society, infidelity and secret love existed, but not like those which occurred at the same period in European kingdoms and occur today in high and low society.

Nurjahan's maiden name was Mehr-un-Nissa. Jahangir, called Prince Saleem before he became Emperor, saw her in the garden and gave her two pigeons to hold in her hands, while he went elsewhere. In the meantime, one bird flew away from her hand. When Jahangir returned, he asked her, "How did the bird fly away?" Letting the other bird also fly away from her hand, most innocently she said that it was this way that the first bird had flown away. Jahangir was struck by her beauty and sincere innocence. On that day he made up his mind to marry her even though his father, Akbar the Great, was against this marital alliance. The father of Mehr-un-Nissa did not permit this marriage either. He was later on appointed as Itimad-ud-Daula, Chancellor of the Exchequer. He wanted to marry his daughter to his nephew Aligul who was afterwards called Sher Afghan as he had killed a tiger with his hands. Even Mehr-un-Nissa, when asked by her father, preferred to marry Aligul. The marriage was performed and the two went away to live in his vast estate in Bengal.

When Jahangir became Emperor after the death of his father, he tried his utmost to get Mehr-un-Nissa to divorce her husband. But every time she sent back the messengers who came to ask for her hand for the Emperor. Her reply was that the King could not use compulsion on his subjects to give up their husbands and go against the laws of the country by marrying them forcibly. Later on, when all chances of taking her as his wife failed, Jahangir plotted with his advisors for the murder of her husband. Jahangir and his conspirators went to a forest to hunt tigers. When a tiger came, Jahangir asked Sher Afghan to fight the tiger with his bare hands. Being proud and having already killed a tiger with his hands, he fought the tiger and, heavily bleeding, himself laid the dead animal at the feet of the Emperor, much to the disappointment of Jahangir.

Later, Kutub-ud-Din, Governor of Bengal, got Sher Afghan killed outside the city where he had called him to meet him. Sher Afghan was living happily in Burdwan with Mehr-un-Nissa and never suspected that the Governor could be treacherous in this way. The Governor got him killed by two servants who accompanied him when he was meeting Sher Afghan a few miles away from Burdwan. It was customary that if the Governor wanted to see any particular individual, he could call him outside the city and, therefore, Sher Afghan never suspected that he would meet the fate that he ultimately did.

Mehr-un-Nissa became a widow and was brought to the Imperial harem at Agra. There Jahangir tried to court her but she never agreed to love Jahangir. She kept some poison and a dagger in her garments, so that if Jahangir tried to rape her she would kill herself.

But Jahangir went on pleading humbly for her love, although in vain. He used to send her bouquets of flowers and love messages which were returned scornfully. As Jahangir had become a lovesick neurasthenic, he neglected the affairs of the State. The Ministers requested Mehr-un-Nissa to accept him as her husband. At the first meeting, the Emperor tried to assure Mehr-un-Nissa that he had no hand in the murder of her husband, but Mehrun-Nissa never believed what he said.

Only after a few years of this meeting, Jahangir got married to Mehr-un-Nissa, giving her the title of 'Nurjahan', the Light of the World. From that time onwards, Nurjahan was the ruler of India while Emperor Jahangir spent his days and nights drinking and merry-making.

It is said that while Jahangir was holding court and making vital decisions regarding his kingdom, Nurjahan would sit behind the throne and place her hand on the back of the Emperor. As long as her hand was there, the Emperor went on deciding case after case submitted to him by his Prime Minister and other Ministers. But the moment the hand was taken away from his back, that was the end of the day's work. Jahangir retired and the Ministers and the courtiers disappeared. Here again, it is crystal clear that Nurjahan was the personification of piety and lofty moral character. Had Sher Afghan not been murdered by the Governor of Bengal, she would have remained faithful to him. For her, wealth and kingdom had no glamour when she was giving her husband the full love of her heart. There are many instances in the history of India from the Epic period to the time of the British rule, where women have shown a lofty moral character and deep fidelity for their husbands. In the later chapters I shall depict Sati and Jauhar which will again reveal to the readers what great sacrifices the women of India were able to make in honour of their husbands when they were facing crushing defeats at the hands of the enemy. When Nurjahan died, the domes under which she was buried were, by her orders, the most unpretentious. Her grave has the most pathetic inscription:

> "On our lone grave let no roses bloom
> Nor a nightingale ever sing
> Let no lamp disperse the gloom
> Nor a moth ever burn its wing."

On Jahangir's tomb it was inscribed:

"Let there not be except green grass
For the mortal poor, this is a
Grave, ever a grave".

Jahangir died in October 1627 in Rajouri on his way back from Kashmir to Delhi.

Even during the long centuries of Muslim Rule in India, one does not hear of any love affairs of the Queens and Princesses, nor has any historian, who visited the Muslim Imperial courts, such as Tavernier and Bernier, mentioned any secret love affairs of the Princesses with any of the relations or any of the Ministers of the State. Mohammedan women were kept in strict *purdah* but they were free to go about without the veil to places which were prescribed. Not a word has been mentioned in history that these Princesses of the Mughal period were unfaithful to their husbands. It is true that if a monarch happened to fall in love with the wife of a nobleman, he went to war against that man, or got him murdered, but never had an Empress any illicit secret connection with any other man while her husband was alive.

29

Mumtaz Mahal — The Lady of the Taj

The story of Mumtaz Mahal runs in the same strain of love and fidelity as of the other Empresses of the Mughal period. She was the Queen of Shahjahan, the Mughal Emperor, and died after living with him happily for long years and giving birth to fourteen children. In commemoration of his love for her, the Emperor built a mausoleum, the Taj Mahal. It is a wonder of the world. Shahjahan had intended to build a similar mausoleum for himself, but in black marble, on the other side of the river Jamuna so that he could be face to face with the Queen even after his death. But his son Aurangzeb captured power and put his father in captivity in the Agra Fort and Shahjahan could not fulfil his desire. He was given a suite of rooms in the Fort facing the Taj. Shahjahan had consolation in watching the tomb day after day though he felt sad looking at the mausoleum which entombed the remains of his beloved. That was the only consolation which Shahjahan had in his captivity — to be able to see the mausoleum of his Queen which was at a distance of a few miles from the Fort of Agra. In order to look at it from near, he had arranged to put some mirrors in his room facing the tomb, through which the image of the mausoleum of Taj

Mahal got reflected and he could see the tomb of his beloved as vividly as if at a distance of a few inches. Shahjahan later on became blind, but he always remembered his wife with great reverence and devotion and the Taj Mahal was of great solace to him in his dying days.

When Shahjahan ascended the throne, Mumtaz Mahal, the Empress, held a unique position in the Imperial Court and the Emperor usually consulted her about private as well as State affairs. She was entrusted with the Royal Seal. After the State documents were finally drafted, they were sent to the Imperial harem and it was her privilege to put the seal on them. This enabled her to get an insight into the current affairs in some of which she took active interest.

30

Concubines at the Helm

Even in the reign of a stern and strict ruler like Aurangzeb, women did exert some influence on politics. Though it appears that Aurangzeb never relished the idea of any interference from his harem, yet sometimes his sisters and daughters exerted some pressure which he did not oppose. During the reign of Jhandar Shanti Lal Kulwar, the famous concubine of the Emperor asserted herself in the affairs of the Empire. She was a dancing girl and possessed no high credentials. Being a favourite of the Emperor, she was allowed some privileges by him. She was allowed to display the Imperial standard and march with drums beating as if she was the Emperor in person. Five hundred gentlemen troopers followed her train. She was also supported by Shah Abdul Gaffar, a *'darvesh'* who became very popular in the harem through his magical powers.

We come across a set of women different from those of the preceding period. Instead of Queens, Princesses or women of high rank, belonging either to the Mughal or Rajput family, there emerged into prominence concubines of low origin — highly ambitious, scheming, self-cantered women — taking advantage of the political crises, spreading tentacles, grasping power and thus undermining beyond all possibility of repair, whatever little moral prestige was still left. It also appears that some of the ladies were anxious to hasten the end of the tottering power of the Emperors. Since they could not do it openly, they did it secretly. Once in A.D. 1611 the Emperor got drunk in the court and was beaten by his own musicians, encouraged by the concubines who had assumed great political power.

In Akbar's time, more than 5,000 women lived in his harem. The number of women increased at the time of Aurangzeb. The highest female servant who controlled the harem was called 'Mahaldar'. She was just like a female Major Domo. She acted as a spy in the interest of the Emperor.

The harem was guarded with great caution. Active women were appointed inside the harem to guard it. Tatar women usually got these posts. The most trustworthy women guards were placed near the apartment of the Emperor, and on the outer fringe, eunuchs were placed at a proper distance. Bands of faithful Rajput guards were deputed at the gate. Besides, on all four sides, there were guards and troops according to their ranks. Nobody could enter the harem. The doors of the harem were closed at sunset and torches were kept burning. Women guards were allowed to send reports to the Nazir of all that happened in the harem. Whenever some women or some nobles desired to visit the harem, they had to first notify the servants of the seraglio and those who were eligible were permitted to enter the harem.

Another interesting feature of the organisation of the harem was that the Emperor appointed similar officers among the fair sex within the palace as he did outside. Some women occupied high offices. Written reports of all the events were sent to the Emperor, which were read in his presence by the women of the palace at about nine o'clock at night. The Emperor was guarded by women skilled in the art of archery and other arms.

31

Valiant Lakshmibai of Jhansi

In ancient India, women wielded much influence in society and played a significant role in various walks of life. They helped their husbands with their wise counsel in moments of crisis. They did not hesitate to take up arms and sacrifice their lives for the honour of their families and the country. In the mediaeval period during the time of Harsha, his sister Rajashri, after the death of her husband, occupied the seat of honour by the side of her brother and also participated in the state deliberations. Even in the Rajput period, administrative training was imparted to promising girls of Rajput families.

At the time of Harsha, women *pratiharis* regulated entry into the palace. Pretty girls were used as *vishakanyas* for the purpose of poisoning enemies.

Rani Lakshmibai, Rani of Jhansi, living up to the grandeur of the old tradition, was another example of the great and chivalrous women of India who never indulged in sexual laxity. Rani Lakshmibai of Jhansi rose head and shoulders above the other women in that epoch. She was born in March 1835 at Banaras and was married early to Subedar G. Rao, head of the small Maria State of Jhansi. The Subedar died without any issue and his widow Lakshmibai was not permitted by the Governor-General in Council to adopt a successor.

John Lang whom she engaged as a lawyer to plead her case before the Directors of the East India Company in England against the decision of the Governor-General in Council, has described her thus: "She was a woman of about middle size, rather stout, but not too stout. She had many charms. Her nose was very delicately shaped." Her appeal was dismissed and Jhansi was taken over by the British Administration. She resolved vengeance and said: "I will not give up Jhansi." On the 5th of June, 1857, rebellion broke out in Jhansi and on the 9th of June, the Rani of Jhansi's authority was proclaimed throughout the State. The Rani stoutly defended the Fort of Jhansi against Sir Hugh Rose. She donned the indomitable *topi* (hat) to lead the troops in military uniform — crimson jacket, crimson trousers and white turban which made it impossible to tell her sex. On the 23rd May of 1858, after a harsh struggle, General Rose captured Kalpi on the river Jamuna about 100 miles east of Jhaola. The Rani of Jhansi in her *topi* fled to the jungle. They attacked again and captured the famous Fort of Sawah on 4th June, 1858.

In the afternoon of the 17th of July, 1858, the Rani was killed in a battle. She received a bullet on the side, and immediately after, a Hussar gave her a cut on the head. She rode off but a moment later, fell down and died.

I have not mentioned the various queens, Maharanis and other great women of India who would rather lose their thrones and kingdoms and perish than lose their chastity. They were both Hindu and Muslim Queens, Maharanis and Begums. In the earlier period the names of Draupadi, Shakuntala, Gandhari, Kunti, Sumitra, Kaushalya and others are worthy of mention.

In the 18th and 19th centuries too there were women whose names could be mentioned as the pride of the civilisation of our country.

32

Napoleon's Faithless Beloved

After writing about the queens, Maharanis and women of India, I would like to give an authoritative account of some of the queens of Europe in the last few centuries, such as Queen Elizabeth of England, Empress Josephine, Empress Marie Louise, Empress Marie Antoinette of France, Empress Catherine II of Russia, and other great women of that epoch. My purpose to show how the moral character of these Queens gradually had a deteriorating effect on the lives of the women of other countries, directly or indirectly.

I will begin with the life of Empress Josephine. She was married to Napoleon Bonaparte, the Emperor of France, on the 9th of March 1796. She was beautiful and full of grace and her *toilette* was the envy of the Parisiennes. She was the widow of General de Beauharnais. French historians record that she had numerous lovers before her marriage to Napoleon and she was known for her *'legerte et prusalites'*. Napoleon often used to write a letter to her from the battlefield. These were the most brilliant letters ever written by a lover to his beloved, and he used to send these through his bodyguards on horseback to

Paris. Josephine was called by the people of France 'Notre Dame des Vietories,' meaning Our Lady of Victory, and the people believed that these victories were due to the presence of this queen. Formerly, she was the mistress of Barras, a great revolutionary who was a Director of the consulate which ruled France after the revolution when Louis XV, Emperor of France, was guillotined. What brought about her fall was her love for young Hyporto Charles. He was so amusing that the queen would not part with him. The people of France began to talk about the love affair of this man with Queen Josephine. When she received love letters full of passion from Napoleon, instead of admiring them, she used to say what a funny man this Napoleon was, thus ridiculing his flaming passion. She came to know the value of these letters only at a later stage.

Napoleon got suspicious about the fidelity of his Queen and asked her to meet him in the battlefield in Italy so that she would be away from the clutches of Charles. In the beginning, she replied that she was unable to join him in the battlefield, giving a thousand excuses, but later she decided to go and meet him. She took Charles with her among her baggage. To the great grief of Napoleon, he found him concealed in one of the big boxes for Josephine's clothes. Napoleon ordered that this man should be handed over to the execution squad, but Josephine came to know of this in time and intervened. She pleaded that this man should be returned to Paris. She promised Napoleon that she would not see him agam. From that day she began to show Napoleon more love, but later Napoleon had to go to Egypt to fight against the Egyptians. During that time Josephine was free to do what she liked and took the opportunity for more love affairs and frivolities. In spite of the promises she had made to Napoleon, she openly began her love affair with the vagabond Hyporto Charles and began to live with him in La Malmaison in Rue Le, which she had purchased in 1798.

Napoleon's brother Joseph informed Napoleon of the infidelity of Josephine and advised him to divorce her.

Napoleon wanted to declare himself as Emperor of France and Josephine as Imperatrice. It was necessary to obtain the approval of Pope Pius VII. Napoleon said: *"La religion est utile au Gouverment. Qui p eut s'en servir pour agir sur les hommes."* Josephine said at the time of her coronation that she would not wish to be married to Napoleon according to Catholic rites and the Pope said that she could not be crowned unless she became a Catholic. Accordingly, Josephine was legally married to Napoleon in accordance with the Catholic religious rites one hour before Napoleon was crowned as Emperor and she as the Empress.

Josephine was a luxury-loving woman. She used to order 520 pairs of shoes in a year, 600 stockings and a similar number of dresses.

She was fond of roses and grew 355 varieties of roses in her magnificent garden of 35 hectares. One still sees the trees planted by Josephine with her own hands. Her bedroom was artistically decorated and her bed had a canopy of velvet and strappings of silk and was three or four rooms away from the bedroom of the. Emperor. It was on this bed that she died after catching a cold while walking in the park with the Tsar of Russia pleading the cause of Napoleon for his return to France from his exile. She was so beautiful, attractive and slender that the Tsar fell for her and promised to consider the proposal and discuss it with his Allies. But fate was against it and she died after three days of pneumonia on the 29th of May 1819, and all her parleys with the Tsar ended with her death. Her mausoleum is erected in the Church of Ruell and her statue decorates the entrance of Bois Preau.

When Napoleon saw the Pope placed on a higher pedestal than himself on the Gurul (Special Chair for the Pope), he said that he was tempted to occupy the Pope's Gurul as he could not tolerate anyone occupying a higher place than himself. Before he died, he said to the person who was taking notes of his last wish: *"Je desire que mes cerdres repoisent sur le bard de de la. Seine au millieu de ce peuple Francais que j'ai tant aime"* (I desire that my remains should be placed on the banks of River Seine in the middle of the French people whom I loved so much). His wish was fulfilled by Emperor Louis Philipe, King of France, who sent a cruiser to bring the last remains of the Great Emperor, and this was 25 years after the death of Napoleon at the age of 37 in the year 1840, on December 21. Just before he breathed his last, Napoleon murmured distinctly and was understood by his servants who surrounded him: *"Mon fils, tete d'Arme Josephine"* (My son head of the Army, Josephine). These were his last words. The British Governor who was specially appointed there to see that Napoleon would not escape from St. Helena as he did from St. Elba, refused to let the word "Emperor" be engraved on his tomb. Afterwards, a magnificent catafalque was built at Hotel des Invalides. This prestigious palace constructed for the glory of the French soldiers who fell in the great war is now the abode of the remains of Napoleon. This great Emperor said, "Love is the occupation of an idler, the amusement of a busy man and the wreck of a sovereign." He once said, "I too was in love — once in life and learned enough of it to despise its definition which only confuses the issue. I deny its justification, nay more, I regard it as injurious to society and destructive to the happiness of the individual. Men should bless heaven if they were devoid of it." Again, he uttered once, "Josephine is always afraid that I may fall seriously in love; she does not realise that love was not made for me. For what is love? A passion that leaves the universe on one side, to place the lover on the other. And surely such an exclusion is not in my character."

It is very interesting to know how Napoleon first met

Josephine when he was 26 years old. She was the wife of a General whose son, Eugene de Beauharnais, came to deliver the only weapon in the house, the sword of his father. Josephine's husband had been guillotined a year before and she herself had been imprisoned and liberated under miraculous circumstances. Napoleon asked Eugene, a young boy of 14 years, why he was crying when he was commanded to deliver his sword in accordance with the ordinance passed by Napoleon for the surrender of all weapons. The young boy explained that this was the sword of his dead father and he would not like to part with it. Napoleon was so impressed by the boy's love for his father and the sword that he allowed him to retain it. Next day, the mother of the boy, Josephine, came to thank him for this favour. The young soldier was used more to the rugged life of the camp than to the sweet society of women. This meeting with Josephine brought a sensation in his heart which he had not felt before. Josephine too fell in love with him at first sight. She was already the mistress of many men, and it was said of her that she would drink gold in the skull of her lover. Napoleon got married to her as instigated and advised by her lover Barras. Although at that time she was 32 and he was 26, in the marriage register both were said to be 29 years old as Napoleon said that love must meet half way.

Napoleon rose from one glory to another, but Empress Josephine failed to produce an heir to the throne and he was ready to divorce her. Napoleon said, "In the 15 years of my life with her, the memory of this will remain for ever stamped in my heart. She was crowned by my hand and I desire that she keeps the rank and the title of crowned Empress but, above all, she will have me as the best and dearest friend." To this Josephine replied, "The dissolution of my marriage will make no change in the sentiments of my heart. The Emperor will always have in me the best friend."

The heavily metalled carriage with four seats inside and a large box outside for the coachman and standing seats for attendants behind the coach, usually used on ceremonial occasions, was sent by Napoleon to take Josephine from the Palace of Tuilleries to Malmaison in Rue Le. She was weeping throughout the long journey of about 40 Km. Since Josephine used this carriage on this occasion, it is known to be lucky and is kept in the stable of Malmaison along with another carriage which Napoleon had used for returning to Paris after his defeat at Waterloo. It is painful to see these two carriages which carried the Emperor and the Empress on these two gloomy and fateful occasions.

Napoleon Bonaparte, 'the greatest general in history,' was a great strategist and had tremendous courage in the battlefield. He won one battle after another, but in his love affairs, particularly with Empress Josephine and Marie Louise, he completely failed. They betrayed him at every step and had lovers known to the people of France. She was the mother of two children and it was Barras who pushed Napoleon into this strange union, all the time smiling cunningly at his own manoeuvring. She married the General Commandant of the Army of Italy. Napoleon, about whom Lazare Camot said, "Bonaparte was brave but very young" wrote to the same Camot from Italy, *"Ma femme ne vient pas, elle a quelque amant qui la retient."* (My wife does not come, she has some lover who retains her in Paris.)

It is of interest to know that about three million votes against 1562 declared Napoleon as the First Consul. Napoleon once said, *"Le difficile nest pas de donner des ordres e'est d'en assurer l'excution."* (It is not so difficult to give orders as to see to their execution.) Therein lay the secret of Napoleon's greatness.

33

Empress Marie Louise and Her Grand Lover

Marie Louise was not only unfaithful and untrue to the Emperor, but, in conspiracy with her father Emperor Francis of Austria, she brought about the downfall and defeat of Napoleon at Waterloo.

After the victory of Napoleon against the Austrians when the Emperor of Austria had to fly from Vienna and the Austrians had to give important territories to France, Metternich, the great Chancellor of Austria, looked for an alliance with the Emperor of the French people. He wrote to the Emperor of Austria, *"I faut que nous reservions nos forces Four les temps meilleure et que nous traveillions et notre salut par des meyons plus dous."* (It is better to reserve our strength for better times. In the meantime, we should work towards the strengthening of our relations with soft and conciliatory methods). Though Archduke Maximilian defended Vienna, yet it fell and Napoleon entered Vienna in the spring of 1809.

Emperor Napoleon had sought the hand of the youngest

sister of Alexander, the Tsar of Russia, who went on delaying the reply to his request. This infuriated Napoleon but Metternich was clever enough to ask the Emperor of Austria to agree to give Napoleon his eldest daughter Grand Duchess Marie Louise in marriage. This flattered Napoleon and the marriage was celebrated in the absence of Emperor Napoleon by Cardinal Feesch, uncle of the Emperor, who blessed the marriage of Napoleon, and Marie Louis. By this act Metternich won the political support of the Emperor of France and Russia lost his friendship.

Napoleon was married officially to Marie Louis at Louvre in Paris. It was not easy for the great house of Hapsburg of Austria which was the oldest and noblest royal family in Europe and had a tradition of being more noble than the Romanoff, to give its daughter to Napoleon who was considered to be an upstart. The marriage was performed in Vienna by proxy.

After Napoleon had beaten the Austrians and entered Vienna, he slept in the Imperial Palace of Schoen-Brunn. Napoleon was careful not to allow any of the sisters of Marie Louise to accompany her to France. They were made to return from the French frontiers. Napoleon did not want that any Austrian should influence her. To the great grief of Marie Louise, even her pet dog was sent back to Vienna.

Marie Louise, puffed up with power as the Empress of France, got fascinated by Adam Albrech, Count Von Neipperg who, as an Austrian officer in 1793, had lost his right eye in a skirmish against the armies of Napoleon in Belgium. He had hatred for Napoleon and was the enemy of the French.

He won the hearts of many women and was known to be a "great lover" in society. Later, he was attached to the Austrians Embassy in Paris and became a Minister in the Court of Sweden.

After Napoleon was exiled to Elba, Marie Louise returned to Vienna and was made Duchess of Parma in Italy. Mepperg and Marie became lovers and were married. Three children were born out of that union.

She was heartless and unfaithful to her great husband Napoleon who was still in love with her when he was exiled to St. Helena. In his Will he spoke of her with great affection and, shortly before his death, said to Antommarchi, his physician, "After my death you will take my heart, put it in the spirit of wine and carry it to Parma to my dear Marie Louise. You will please tell her that I tenderly loved her and that I never ceased to love her. You will relate to her all that you have seen."

When cruel Marie Louise was told the news of the final exile of Napoleon to St. Helena, she observed, "Thanks — by the way I should like to ride this morning to Markenstein. Do you think that the weather is good enough to make it?"

34

The Insatiable Christina of Sweden

In the battle of Lutzen in Saxony, Gustaws Adolphus, King of Sweden, died after receiving a mortal blow. His daughter Christina was made Queen of Sweden at the age of six. Christina was crowned at the age of eighteen, but in spite of the ardent wishes of the people of Sweden, she refused to marry. After her ascent to the throne she ruled with an iron hand. In 1648, she fought the thirty-year war which ended with the treaty called the Peace Treaty of Westphalia. People know of the slander regarding her moral character. She had lovers from all parts of Europe. A French physician named Bourdelet was her first lover. She would not spend her time in love-making in the ordinary sense. Like Mussolini, she demanded brutal satisfaction from her ardent lovers. She believed in brutal licentiousness. But she was a good and strong ruler and showed her prowess in the battlefield and in administration, and as such the people of Sweden ignored her sex adventures in the beginning, but later on when the scandal about her adventures rose to the highest peak, the people began to look down upon her. She, therefore, declared her cousin Charles as an heir to Sweden, had him crowned, and abdicated in his favour.

Thereafter, she went to Rome and was received by Pope Alexander VII, baptized and given the new name of Alexandra. In Rome she fell in love with Marquis Monaldeschi. From Rome she went to Paris, where she was lovingly treated by Louis XIV, the King of France. There Christina took another lover by the name of Sentanelli, an Italian by nationality, who was Captain of her Guard.

Monaldeschi became extremely jealous and betrayed the Queen by divulging her secrets to Oliver Cromwell, going to the extent of forging her signature and the seal of Sentanelli and sending to Oliver Cromwell scandalous letters about Christina. Christina, quick-witted as she was, recognised the source of these letters and was sure that Monaldeschi was at the bottom of the plot in despatching the secret letters. It was recorded by historians that Christina showed these letters to Monaldeschi. She asked him to confess that these letters were sent by him. Monaldeschi broke down and begged pardon of the Queen. The Queen told him, "You are my subject and for me you are a traitor and so, Monaldeschi, you must prepare yourself to die." The Queen had retained the powers of life and death over her subjects before abdicating. Then the Guards of Queen Christina approached him with drawn swords and one of the Guards cut the forehead of Marquis Monaldeschi and another Guard put a sword across his side and the Marquis fell, mortally wounded. When Father Label, the Queen's Household Chaplain, went to the Queen's apartment and informed her of what had happened, she was ready to 'justify' herself. She said that she was still a monarch with full powers to treat traitors at her will.

Subsequently, Christina tried to regain the throne but it was refused by the people. Then she returned to Rome where she was royally received by the Pope. She died at the age of 53 and was buried in St. Peters.

35

Anne Boleyn Meets Her Fate

Anne Boleyn was the Second Queen of Henry VIII of England. She was the daughter of Sir Thomas Boleyn and of Elizabeth, daughter of Thomas Howard, Earl of Surrey, who was afterwards given the title of Duke of Norfolk. Anne was well-known in the English Court and had the opportunity of meeting King Henry VIII, who fell in love with her and wrote to her the most passionate love letters before he married her. The impasse about her marriage with the King was due to the King's marriage with Catherine of Aragon which had to be annulled before he could marry Anne. The King was determined to get rid of Catherine, not only because she could not produce a son for him who was to be the male heir to the throne, but also because she was growing old and was ailing and the King was attracted to Anne most passionately. After Henry's final separation from Catherine in July 1531, Henry secretly married Anne and the union was made public the following Easter on March 28. Archbishop Granmer pronounced the marriage valid and that of Catherine null and void.

In June, Anne was crowned and in September she gave

birth to a daughter who became the future Queen Elizabeth of England. The birth of a daughter was a great disappointment to Henry whose love for Anne began to fade away gradually year by year as she was unable to produce a male heir to the throne.

She was later accused of the charge of adultery with various men, including her own brother Lord Kochford, Sir Francis Weston, Henry Morris, William Brereton and Mark Samenton. They were tried and found guilty of high treason as her lovers.

Three days later, Anne and her brother were condemned unanimously by a Court of 26 peers presided over by her uncle the Duke of Norfolk as Lord Steward. On May 17, her reputed lovers were executed and Granmer pronounced her marriage with Henry invalid. Anne was beheaded in the Tower Green on May 19, meeting her death with courage and even with a jest.

Though Anne was not described as a woman of great beauty, yet her dark and beautiful eyes had attracted Henry VIII. She had a wide mouth and her bosom was not big. She was of a middle stature but she had a great hold on the King, whom she sometimes treated harshly and even with contempt.

On the other hand, Henry VIII was the first monarch to be educated under the influence of the cultural renaissance and his tutors included the poet John Skeleton. He became an accomplished scholar, linguist, musician and athlete.

The death of his elder brother Arthur made him heir apparent and, in 1503, he was engaged to Arthur's widow, Catherine of Aragon. His father, however, delayed the marriage and even protested against it while some doubts were expressed about its validity in Canon Law. Nevertheless, Henry VIII married Catherine on the 22nd of April, 1509, after his accession. The marriage of Anne with Henry VIII brought about the greatest revolution in the Church. Pope Clement VII was opposed to the divorce of Catherine and the marriage with Anne. In order to have his own way and to be able to marry Anne, King Henry VIII abolished Papal jurisdiction and caused the Parliament to pass a series of Acts of the most momentous consequence. The clergy was brought completely under his control. He was acknowledged as the Supreme Head of the Church of England, and it was made high treason to deny his title and authority. Thus the King boldly and resolutely retaliated against the Pope by repudiating his supremacy in England and by clothing himself with ecclesiastical powers. The King encouraged the movement launched by Martin Luther, the Protestant reformer, who denied the spiritual supremacy of the Pope and the central dogma of transubstantiation on which much of the Pope's priestly power depended.

As Henry flouted the Pope's authority, he removed all obstacles to the divorce of Catherine and legalisation of Henry's marriage with Anne.

After Thomas Cromwell, the Earl of Essex, was beheaded, Anne too was divorced and beheaded. Henry then married Jane Seymour in order that he may have a son from her, as he was infatuated with the idea that he must have a male heir to the throne.

Henry VIII has been described as a despot under the forms of Law, and it is apparently true that he committed no illegal act. His despotism did not consist in ruling unconstitutionally, but he was able to use constitutional means for the fulfilment of his personal ends.

Henry could thus behead Ministers and divorce wives with comparative impunity. He was the remorseless incarnation of Machiavelli's Prince. He had an elastic conscience. It was always at the beck and call of his desires and he cared little for principles.

Anne Boleyn, like many other queens of England, France, Russia and other countries of Europe, was a sexual fiend and admitted to the King before she was beheaded that not only was she having sexual relations with the great nobles of the realm but did not spare the military guards of her palace either.

It is most interesting for the readers to see from the above narration that in spite of the fact that the King made her the Queen of England and bestowed upon her all his love, she was in passionate love with many other men who were afterwards executed for being found in flagrant 'delit' with the Queen. The law of England at that time prescribed death sentence for adultery.

The stories of Anne and other queens of Europe were widely known in India and other Asiatic countries, and inspired Indian women, particularly the Maharanis and women in the higher strata, to act in a similar way.

36

Catherine of Russia, the Callous Beloved

The queens of Russia, like other women of Asia and other countries, covered their faces in public, particularly before the reign of Peter the Great.

Catherine II the Great, known as Le Semiramis de Nord, Empress of Russia, reigned after the death of her husband Peter III from 1762 to 1790. She fought alone, and successfully, the wars against the Turks, Poland, Ukraine and Ltune.

After the death of Empress Elizabeth, it was Peter the Great who brought women out of seclusion and made them take part in parties and balls.

On political considerations, Catherine, like the other queens in Europe, had to take a lover to have a son, as her husband was sexless. A son was indeed born to Catherine. But this boy was taken away from her as soon as he was born. After the death of Empress Elizabeth in 1761, Peter became the Tsar of Russia. He was an imbecile and did not even pay proper homage to the corpse of the late Empress. He declared that the day he divorced Catherine, all the courtiers would also divorce their wives and take new wives. He beat the guard and became unbalanced and whimsical and the result was that the people revolted against him. Knowing that Catherine had become very popular with the people, Peter wanted to arrest Catherine as her popularity was undermining his own prestige in the kingdom. She appealed to the Army for her safety and one regiment after another resided with her. A few soldiers gathered around her. The Emperor had given orders to arrest Catherine. Catherine had a lover, Gregory Orlov, who murdered Peter, and thus she became the Empress.

There was another man by the name of Potemkin who had lost his heart to her and longed to be her lover. A struggle started between Gregory Orlov and Potemkin over the love of the Empress. When Orlov came to know that Potemkin was gaining the love of the Empress, he became abusive and attacked Potemkin who lost his eye in the scuffle. This was a turning point in the life of Potemkin. The Empress allowed Potemkin to write love letters to her. In the meantime, Orlov was not allowed to enter the city of Gath. The Queen took another lover, Wassiltchikov. On the other hand, Potemkin suffered terribly out of jealousy, and retired to a monastery. This melted the heart of the Empress who asked him to come back. She installed him as the Secretary to the Empress and her lover and dismissed Wassiltchikov. The Empress decorated him with the highest order of the Empire and confessed to Potemkin that she had only had four lovers before him. Being a temperamental and unbalanced man and being inconsistent with his love, he got jealous of Orlov when the Empress met him at a theatre and said a few nice words to him. He completely changed his way of life with the Empress. They decided to live together, but both of them would be free to seek love elsewhere and in political affairs would collaborate as before.

This ardent lover Potemkin brought her new lovers and made it very clear to the Empress that his approval would be necessary before she changed any lover and that any lover could also be dismissed by him. In other words, he did not want any lover to have political ascendancy. He wanted to keep the power in his hands.

He died on the roadside on his way to Moldavia, and in his pocket were found notes and letters of Catherine which he carried with him throughout his life.

37

Marie Antoinette in the Death Chamber

Following a decree of the Convention which sent her before the Revolutionary Tribune, Marie Antoinette was guillotined on the 16th of October 1793. This ill-fated queen, the consort of King Louis XVI, spent the last days of her life at the Conciergerie which was once turned into a palace under the reign of Philippele-Bel (Philip IV, the Fair), at the end of the XIIIth or the beginning of the XIVth century. It was turned into a prison during the great revolution.

It will be interesting for the readers to know the brief history of Conciergerie. It is its archaeological construction which makes the Conciergerie the most remarkable specimen of French civil architecture in the middle ages. Its towers and magnificent rooms were an integral part of the princely dwelling which the monarchy abandoned at the request of the Parliament in the XIVth century. The monarchy left it in the care of the Palace Concierge (caretaker) who was an important person endowed with privileges and wide powers. The name had a triple meaning. It was sometimes applied to the Concierge's own house, sometimes to the King's dwelling, and sometimes to the prison attributed to the Concierge's jurisdiction, and later put at the disposal of the Parliament. It is in this prison that Marie Antoinette was brought from 'Donjon du Temple' where she was imprisoned during the fateful night of August 12.

A little more than five months had passed since the execution of Louis XVI. The Royal family had been taken to this tower near the Palais du Grand Prieur nearly a year before, after the capture of the Tuileries and the fall of the monarchy. There remained only three persons: Louis XVII separated from his mother a month before, his sister Marie-Therese-Charlotte destined to survive her family, and their aunt Madame Elizabeth.

The Convention's decree did not mean that the Queen's fate was definitely decided. In fact, the Comite de Salut Public (the Committee for Public Welfare) of the Convention hoped to use the Queen, who was the Emperor of Austria's sister and daughter of the late Empress Marie-Therese, as a pawn to bring about the end of the war with Austria. The sudden decision and rumours of a quick judgment and the prompt execution that the Comite adroitly spread were meant only to hasten the anticipated negotiations. However, the foreign powers did not move. Only a few devout Royalists worked to bring about an escape. The best known of these attempts was to be the 'Affaire de l' Oeillet' (the Carnation Affair) which almost succeeded. It was only then that the Convention's hopes for peace were destroyed and feeling the weight of its responsibilities, the Comite de Salut Publiqe met at a secret session on September 2, and decided on the death of the Queen as well as other serious and salutary measures.

Marie Antoinette arrived at the Conciergerie around 3 in the morning. She was charged in her cell. The heat was stifling. "The prisoner's face was covered with drops of perspiration which she wiped two or three times with her handkerchief."

The assistants left. The wife of the Concierge Richard and her servant Rosalie Lamorliere offered their services to the prisoner. She refused them. She hung her watch on a hook, the gold watch which she brought from Germany when she came to be the Dauphine.

Then she prepared herself for the night. She slept in a bed "made with fine linen sheets and a pillow." The second and the hardest and most painful part of her life as a captive began.

Situated not far from the clerk's office between the third and fourth gates at the end of a "long dark corridor", Marie Antoinette's first cell at the Conciergerie looked out on to the women's courtyard "through two little windows almost on the level of the pavement." It was called the 'Sane du Consal des gaoliers' (the Jailer's Council Room). According to G. Lenotre, it could be the room called "La Cechot de la Valette" (Valet's Cell).

In any case, the Queen's life in the "Council Room" was rigidly organised. In the beginning, an eighty-year-old woman, warden Larivier's mother, was put at her service. It was not long before she was judged 'not fit' for this employment. So she was replaced by a young woman named Harel whose husband was employed at the police headquarters. For this reason, the Queen almost never spoke to her.

Marie Antoinette's breakfast was served at nine o'clock and her lunch at two or two-thirty. The first meal consisted of coffee or chocolate and a small rye bread. For lunch, she was given soup, a plate of boiled beef, a plate of vegetables, chicken or veal and a dessert served in pewter-ware. This customary fare was later reduced. The supper was composed of leftovers from dinner. Without being refined, the food was at least "healthy and suitable." "The Queen," reported Rosalie Lamorliere twenty-five years later, "ate with good appetite; she cut her chicken into two, so it would last two days. She picked the bones with unbelievable ease and care. She scarcely left enough vegetables for a second serving... She drank only water, even at Versailles, as she reminded us sometimes."

Rising early, she dressed immediately. Her hair-do since her arrival at the Conciregerie, was the simplest — she parted her hair on the forehead after having put a bit of scented powder in it. Mme. Harel tied the ends of her hair together with a piece of white ribbon, wound it up and then gave the end of the ribbon to Madame, who crossed them herself and fastened them on the top of her head, giving het hair (blonde, not red) the form of a loose chignon. Later, because of the attitude of a new Concierge, she had to do her hair without help. She gratefully received a mirror brought to her in secret. Its frame was red and "Chinese style figures" were painted on both sides. Purchased on the quais, it cost only 25 sous of Revolutionary money called 'assignats'.

When she came to the Conciergerie, the Queen "had brought no kind of clothing or garments with her." The next day and the following day she repeatedly asked for clothing. Because of the fear of being implicated, no one dared lend or give anything to her. Finally, a municipal servant who "at heart was an honest man" went over to the Temple prison and brought back a bundle which was promptly opened. It contained some beautiful batiste chemises, handkerchiefs, scarves, black silk or floss stockings, a white dressing gown for the morning, a few night caps and several pieces of ribbon of unequal width." This clothing was taken away after the "Carnation Affair" and afterwards Marie Antoinette was given "her chemises one by one." Through Mme Richard, the Queen succeeded in having her large widow's head-dress cut, and, the abundance of material in it served to make her two morning bonnets.

She wore, hung around her neck by a cord or hidden in her corset, the portrait of her son and a lock of his hair wrapped in a little yellow kid glove which had belonged to the child. Often she concealed herself near her camp-bed to kiss these relics tearfully.

Her black dress, the only dress she could wear alternately with the white dressing gown, was falling in tatters, worn out by use and humidity. Concierge Bault's daughter sewed a new edging on it. Thanks to some unknown devotee, Marie Antoinette received some warm stockings made by the Sisters of Charity de-Saint-Roch towards the end of her captivity. Pieces of these stockings, heavily-lined, were used to identify the remains of the Queen during the exhumation at the Cemetery of the Madeleine in 1814.

There was no pen, ink, or paper at Marie Antoinette's disposal. To occupy herself during the long days until the evening when deprived of the lamp and the "torch", she had only the feeble light reflected from the lamp in the women's courtyard for getting into the bed. The Queen sometimes read. She read and re-read the few books which the Concierge lent her — "The Voyages of Captain Cook", "Young Anacharsis" and "English Revolution". At one time she found a way to pull out several threads in the rough tapestry which hung on the wall and to braid "a sort of garter" or lace by using toothpicks and pins. This was to be given to her daughter MarieTherese-Charlotte when she was "exchanged" for deputies or Republican agents who were Austrian agents or prisoners.

Often Marie Antoinette played automatically with her wedding ring and two pretty diamond rings; she took them off, put them on, and passed them from one hand to the other several times in a moment. These jewels were taken away by two dubious characters during the search for the "Carnation Affair".

She watched distractedly the card game of the gendarmes who guarded her.

Since Marie Antoinette was to be under constant watch, she had to endure the presence of two gendarmes who spent their time "drinking, playing cards and smoking separated from her by only a small screen."

This fact made more difficult the execution of the hopeful projects of several Royalists, generally of humble origin, who feverishly made plans to bring about the Queen's escape.

The most important of these attempts, if not the most well-known (although numerous points of the episode remain obscure) was the "Carnation Affair" ('L' Affaire de l' Oeillet').

The organiser of the Affair was the Marquis de Rougeville. Since G. Lenotre's historical discoveries, we know that he was not a Marquis and that his name was Gonsse. But this has little importance. Son of a newly-rich farmer, he said that he took part in the American Revolutionary War. When he returned, he was among the last defenders of the monarchy. Rougeville, who was quite a mysterious personality, had the bold idea of securing the help of several men, provoking a tumult or riot and taking advantage of this to abduct the Queen. It was, however, indispensable to warn Marie Antoinette, to convince her to flee and to permit her to neutralise her attendants.

Resolutely, Rougeville began to execute his plan. He managed to become friendly with a café-keeper, Michonis, who had become administrator of the prison. Using curiosity as a pretext, he succeeded in penetrating into the Queen's cell with him on the 28th August 1793.

Marie Antoinette recognised Rougeville instantly. With a gesture, he indicated the carnation which decorated the buttonhole of his grey suit, took off the flower and threw it behind the stove. As soon as he had left, the Queen distracted the attention of the gendarmes for a moment and picked up the flower. It contained a note with words of hope and offers of money After having read it, she tore up the message. Using a pin, Marie Antoinette traced a reply on a fragment of curl-paper which was lying about. Trembling, she hastened to play her role. She had noticed gendarme Gilbert's gentleness and decent manner. She spoke to him, showed him the note that she had just written and let him take it. Anxious to respect his orders, gendarme Gilbert, six days later on the 3rd of September, related the incident in a weekly report to his Colonel fearing that he would "compromise the whole corps."

Thus warned, the 'Comite de salut Public,' sent three of its members to the Conciergerie to open an investigation. The Queen was forced to submit to a long and meticulous questioning. In vain did they examine Marie Antoinette's reply to the message of which a facsimile exists in a show-case of the little museum situated in the former chapel. Towards the end of the 19th century, it was deciphered as:

Je ne parle a' personne'	I speak to no one
Je suis gardes a' vue'	I am constantly guarded
Je viendrais'	I shall come

The principal results of the Carnation Affair were the imprisonment of Michonis as well as one of his associates and the sentencing of the Richard couple to hard labour. Rougeville escaped search. Perhaps the Carnation Affair also hastened the trial and conviction of Marie Antoinette which were decided on the 2nd of September. In any case, the captive's regimen became more strict. "Several visits were made in her little room. Her drawer was opened, she herself was searched, her chairs and bed were overturned. Routine visits took place after that at any hour of the day or night, architects and administrators verified the solidity of the iron bars and the walls at every instant." Finally, another cell farther away from the door of the prison was chosen.

Nothing resembles less its former state than the Queen's cell as it exists today. To the almost complete alteration of the cell itself, one should add the current stories and traditions which have resulted in modifying the truth. For example, it is inexact to say that the door of the cell was lowered to force Marie Antoinette to bow down. The origin and authenticity of the door story are open to doubt. If the Queen had the possibility of receiving communion in her cell, the scene in all likelihood does not correspond to that shown in a painting hung in the cell. If there are not many features of the original state of the cell left, we can at least suppose without fear of error that the brick floor-tiles existed as early as September and October 1793.

We owe to the Restoration and its political shrewdness or its piety this transformation of the Queen's cell and its heavy and pretentious expiatory altar.

In order to obtain these results, they busied themselves in walling up certain portions, opening up another one, replastering the walls, remaking the ceiling made of beams and joists, enlarging the window of blue and yellow diamond shapes with most disconcerting effects.

Before the Queen's cell was used as a pharmacy, this square and quite a large room had two windows. One looked out on the women's courtyard and the other on the infirmary. A document kept at the National Archives specifies that the first window "was blocked up to the fifth horizontal bar by a piece of sheet iron 1.12 of an inch thick. The rest was covered with a very closely woven iron grille. The second window was entirely blocked up. Another window of the corridor was also entirely blocked."

The cell was divided into two equal parts by means of partition. An open space was left in front of which a low screen was placed.

On entering, the left part was reserved for gendarmes. They slept there on a camp-bed. In the right section, reserved for Marie Antoinette were placed a camp-bed and a mattress, a table with drawers, a stool covered with inexpensive material, two prison chairs and utensils for a variety of uses. The time when they managed to put fine linen sheets on the bed and a vase of flowers on the table had passed.

A question can be asked here. Did the Queen receive communion in this cell as she did in the first one? The texts must be examined in order to determine this date from the Restoration, the epoch when "the Austrian" or "the Capetian widow" had once again become this "great princess", and the august "victim". More or less each person who was employed at the Conciergerie, if not everybody, affirms that he risked his life to obtain aid and help for the Queen. Although it does not seem exempt from certain contradictions, a solemn declaration that Abbey Magnin, Priest of the Saint-Germain l' Auxerrois parish, made in 1825 confirms the facts. Thanks to the charitable old lady, Mlle. Fouche, and the complicity of the Concierie Richard and then the Concierge Dault, Marie Antoinette is supposed to have received communion several times at the Conciergerie; at first from the hands of Abbey Magnin and then, during the night of October 12-13, 1793, from M. Cholet, a priest from Vendee.

This last date corresponds to about the moment the Queen was warned of her approaching appearance before the Court, from the conversation held intentionally under her window.

It is not necessary to relate the trial of Marie Antoinette here, nor the debates which lasted about 20 consecutive hours during which numerous witnesses were heard. It is probable that the Queen kept up some hope until the last moment. The severity of the sentence, which could scarcely be avoided, seemed to surprise her. However, she gave not the "slightest sign of fear, nor indignation, nor weakness," reported Chauveau Lagarde, her Counsel. She was as if overwhelmed by surprise. She descended the steps without uttering a word or making a gesture, crossed the room, seemed to see nothing and hear nothing, and when she arrived in front of the barrier which kept back the public, she raised her head majestically.

After her conviction, Marie Antoinette had to go back to her usual cell towards four in the morning. However, according to some testimony, she was brought "to an office through the entry to the Clerk's office." This does not seem to agree with the principal accounts.

It was then that she drew up the letter to Madame Elizabeth, known as the *"Testament de la Reine"* (The Queen's Testament), and she wrote several lines on a prayer book now at the library of Chalons-sur-Mame. The authenticity of these two texts has been contested without any decisive proof.

Towards eleven in the morning, Rosalie Lamorliere went down to the cell where two lamps were burning and saw the Queen dressed all in black, lying on the bed. She wanted to bring her some "beef broth and noodles", which Marie Antoinette refused. Later she accepted the broth of which she could swallow only two or three spoonfuls. Afflicted with a violent loss of blood, she went into the narrow space between her bed and the wall to resign herself to remaining under the watchful eye of the gendarme officer who refused her request "in the name of honesty to change her clothes without witnesses." The Queen sighed. She put on her last chemise with all the precaution and modesty possible. She chose as a dress the white dressing gown which she wore in the morning and crossed her large muslin scarf round her neck, after having knotted a black silk favour around her wrist.

They came to read the sentence to her again. Henry Sanson, the Executioner's son, entered. He cut her hair. At eleven she entered the Executioner's cart where she was made to turn her back to the horse. A priest was by her side. She ignored him. Detachments of gendarmes, mounted and on foot, formed the procession which advanced slowly. The Queen appeared before the crowds, her hair all white and close-cropped... her face pale and a little red-cheeked, her eyes blood-shot and her eyelashes unmoving and stiff. It is thus the famous sketch by David, done from a window in the rue Saint Honore, shows her. While going from the palace to the foot of the scaffold, she looked "calmly on the innumerable people who shouted *"Vive la Republique"* (Long Live the Republic).

Upon arriving at the Place de la Revolution (Place de la Concorde) her eyes fixed "with some sensitivity on the Tuileries Palace."

She got down lightly from the cart and submitted herself to the preparations for her death. At precisely a quarter past twelve her head fell. It was the 16th of October 1793.

In this historical prison, a lot of atrocities were committed. One cannot believe that such third degree methods and cruelty were possible in France.

After Ravaillac struck Henri IV on the 14th May of 1610 when he was passing in a carriage along Rue de la Ferronerie, he was quickly disarmed and brought to the Hotel de Ritz near Louvre where he was imprisoned at the Conciergerie. His trial began on the 27th. Before being executed in 'the Place de

Greve' he had to submit to torture. He was inflicted with the punishment of the "brodequins". Four planks of oak were put on the legs, holes permitted cords to be held in readiness, which the torturer pulled tightly around the planks. Four wooden wedges were driven with blows from a hammer from below, one after the other between the planks and the knee. For worse torture, more wedges were hammered in. Called upon to denounce his supposed accomplices, Ravaillac at the first wedge asked God to have pity upon his soul; at the second wedge, he declared himself to be a sinner and to know nothing else; at the third, he fainted. He was revived end laid out on a mattress before being brought to the Saint Chapelle, where he was admonished again and then brought to the execution ground.

There he was tortured with red hot pincers, burned with fire and brimstone, sprinkled with hot lead, boiling oil, pitch burning resin, wax and brimstone melted together, and then pulled apart and dismembered by four horses, his limbs and body consumed by fire and reduced to ashes which were thrown to the winds.

When Louis XV, the descendant of Henri IV, was struck and lightly wounded by Damiens, another fanatic, on the 5th of January 1757 at Versailles, the treatment inflicted on Ravaillac became the inspiration for Damiens' punishment.

It was not until the night of January 18th that a detachment of the French Guard brought in the prisoner. The procession quickly reached the Conciergerie, crossing the deserted streets where it was forbidden for the *bourgois* to be at the windows.

Damiens' cell was situated on the second floor of the big tower, the Tower of Montgomery, which evoked the memory of the involuntary murderer of Henri II, the Comte de Montgomery, who stayed here for so many years. It was torn down in 1778.

For sixty days, Damiens remained attached to a sort of cot tied down by thongs of Hungarian leather which were held by twenty rings fastened to the floor. Four seargents watched him continuously. He received the "brodequins" torture after his conviction on the 29th of March, 1757. His punishment was conducted with strange refinements of cruelty which surpassed the circumstances of his execution. It took place before the eyes of a multitude of the curious, as numerous as the crowds present in 1678 at the execution of one of the most famous prisoners ever known, the Marquis de Brinvilliers, or as those present in 1721 at the execution of Cartouche, killer and robber, whose sinister exploits have become legendary.

38

Blessed be the Dead

In prehistoric times there prevailed a belief in several societies that the life and needs of the dead in the next world are more or less similar to those in this life. It, therefore, became a pious duty of the surviving relations to provide a dead person all that he usually needed when alive, and specially when an important person like a king, a nobleman or a warrior died, it was felt that the usual paraphernalia should be sent with him as we find in the Egyptian pyramid. He would, of course, require his horses, his servants and his women in the next world and it would therefore be reasonable and desirable to kill all these who formed the entourage. Such a belief could have given rise to the custom of burning the husband also along with the wife.

The custom of sacrificing the widow at the funeral of the husband was widely prevalent in ancient times. It was prevalent among the Gulas, Goths, Norwegians, Celts, Slavs. It was probably well established among the Scythians. In China, if a widow killed herself in order to follow her husband to heaven, the corpse was taken out in a big procession.

This custom made the life of the Patriarch very safe, as

it practically eliminated all possibilities of anyone among his numerous and mutually envious women intriguing against his life. They all knew that, even if successful, they had no chance of surviving him. Therefore, they all cared to see that there was no accident to the husband's life. It was argued that this custom had Vedic sanction. It was mentioned in the funeral hymn in the Veda that the first two widows had ascended the funeral pyre.

We cannot conclude from it that the 'Sati' as a custom was recognised as a ritual in the Vedic period. In the period 700 to 800 A.D., 'Sati' became very frequent in northern India and quite common in Kashmir. The history of Kashmir during this period depicts the cases of 'Sati' in the Royal family.

It was due to piety, faithfulness and devotion to the husband that Indian women performed the 'Sati' ritual.

39

Self-immolation as a Tradition

It is a well-known fact that "Sati" and 'Johar' had been practised in India' from time immemorial. Western people and many Asiatics think that these were barbarous customs of the Hindus and had been forced upon the women of this country. None truly gauges the truth of these customs as performed by the women of India. One marvels at the sacrifices which they made, and if one knew how and in what circumstances 'Sati' and 'Johar' were performed, one would realise that it was not by compulsion on the part of men that women burnt themselves along with their husbands or burnt themselves alone when faced by enemies who would forcibly capture them and use them as concubines.

The practice of 'Sati' can be traced to mythology. There are many heart-rending accounts of women sacrificing their lives in 'Sati' and 'Johar' ceremonies.

Under the intrepid Maharaja Jaswant Singh Rathore, 30,000 Rajput Chiefs of his clan advanced to the junction of the armies under the cover of artillery commanded by Frenchmen and crossed the river almost unopposed. The Rajputs behaved in the usual brave manner, but were surrounded on all sides by the enemy troops. By sunrise they had left 10,000 dead in the field. The Maharaja retreated and returned to his capital, but his wife, the daughter of Maharaja Rana of Udaipur, disdained to receive her runaway lord and shut the gates of the castle.

Bernier, the great French writer and traveller who was present, says: "I cannot forbear to relate the fierce reception which the daughter of the Maharaja Rana gave to her husband Jaswant Singh after his defeat and flight. She commanded in a dry mood the shutting of the gates of the castle and not letting this infamous man enter, for he was not worthy to be her husband and the son-in-law of the great Rana after having behaved so cowardly in the battle."

The Maharani sent word to her husband that he was either to conquer or to die. The Rana returned to the battlefield with his shattered forces and was killed. Later, she was all in good humour. She commanded a pile of wood to be laid that she might burn herself, believing that her husband must be dead and that she could not remain alive. "A pattern of the courage of the women in their country!" so says Monsieur Bernier.

The names of Rana Pratap, Maharana Sanga and Rani Padmini are well-known in the golden annals of chivalry and deathless sacrifice and will ever remain enshrined in Indian hearts and history.

THE MARTYR QUEEN OF GANORE

The beauty of the Queen of Ganore was an allurement only secondary to the Khan's desire for this country. The Khan awaited her in the hall below. She said she would be ready in two hours to receive him. The Queen told the courtiers to receive him and to dress well. She would take two hours to dress. When the Khan was ushered into the hall of the palace, the Queen was found dead in her beautiful clothes. These clothes were made for an occasion such as this when the Queen would find herself in a desperate situation. Special poisons were secretly placed on the inner side of the dress which caused instantaneous death by their touch.

The influence of women in society is impressed on every page of Indian history. What had led to the wars of Lord Rama? It was the forced and unwilling abduction of Sita. What had made the Pandavas fight the Kauravas? It was the insult to Draupadi. What had made Nala an exile from Nishadh? It was his love for Damayanti. What had made Raja Bhiryhi abandon the throne of Awanti? It was the loss of Pingayi and the rape of the princesses of Camout.

THE 'JOHAR' AT CHITTORE

The fatal ceremony of 'Johar' was commanded and 8,000 Rajput ate the last 'birra' (betel leaf) together and put on their saffron robes; the gates were thrown open, the destruction in battle commenced and few survived. For, they would not stain the sanctity of their yellow mantle with the unholy tar of abject surrender.

Emperor Akbar entered Chittore only when 30,000 of its inhabitants had become victims of his ambitious thirst for conquest. All the heads of the clan fell and 1,700 of the immediate kin of the princesses along with their Queens, five princesses with their infant sons and the families of all the chieftains perished in the flames on this ever-memorable day. Akbar estimated the volume of destruction from the quantity of the sacred threads taken from the necks of the valorously dead Rajputs, which weighed 74 *maunds* and-a-half, i.e., nearly three tons.

HISTORIC 'JOHAR' AT LONI

One of the greatest 'Johars' in history took place at Loni which is situated in Uttar Pradesh in Tehsil Ghaziabad. This small town is today linked with Ghaziabad and Shahdara by metalled roads on one side and with Delhi via Wazirabad and other bridges on the other side. The fort at Loni is said to date from the time of Prithvi Raj, King of Delhi, in the last quarter of the 12th century. Local traditions show that in the 11th century, the north of the district was held by Tages. They were driven to the south and east by the Jats who had entered the district in the north and west, and thus spread themselves over the Parganas that they now occupy. In the south were the Meos and to the south-west the Dors, of which the traditional leader was Raja Hari Dutt. The Dors were expelled by the Gahlots with the help of the Meos.

Loni town formed part of the villages which were offered by Duryodhana, King of the Kauravas, to King Yudhisthira of the Pandavas — Talpat, Sonepat, Bhaget, Loni and Indraprastha in the time of the *Mahabharata* — and is at present a small town of about 5,000 inhabitants on the road to Saharanpur and Ghaziabad on the other side. Recently, a club called the Orient and Occident Union Club was built on a hilltop with a picturesque view of magnificent pastures and of Delhi and the neighbouring towns. It is in this club that people of the West and the East meet to cement the ties of friendship between themselves and their countries. I am the Founder-President of this Club.

In 1738, Taimur invaded Meerut and captured it. Marching from Kaithal, Taimur came to Panipat and thence by Khani Gasin to the Jamuna where he discovered on the opposite side the fort and town of Loni, then held by one Maimum on behalf of Sultan Mahmood. This is mentioned in the autobiography Zafar Nama of Yazdi. He describes Loni as situated between the two rivers Jumna and Halin, the latter being a large canal which was cut from the river Kalindi and brought to the Ferozabad bank connected with the Jamuna by Feroz Shah. The garrison appears to have been of Hindus attached to the faction of Mallu Khan, the Hindu Minister of Mahmood Shah.

Pastures being scant on the Delhi side of the river, Taimur crossed the river while Maimum made preparations for resistance. Taimur relates that a Holy Sheikh came out of the town and said that he had made the utmost endeavours to induce the people to surrender but that they had remained obstinate. Taimur ordered an assault which was successful. Many of the Rajputs placed their wives and children in their houses and burnt them and then rushed into the battle to be killed. Taimur goes on to relate how he gave orders for the safety of all Muslims and indiscriminate slaughter of all Hindus in the town and the fort and thence he marched along and took up his quarters opposite Delhi. His principal officers represented that they had 1,000 prisoners in the camp and that in the event of all the forces being required to attack Delhi, they would find it difficult to give assistance as they were guarding the prisoners. Thereupon, Taimur ordered that all the prisoners be massacred, and so much was this in consonance with the advice of his spiritual counsellors that we read of a holy Maulvi who had never killed a sparrow in his life, slaying fifteen Hindus who were assigned to him as captives and as his share of the spoil.

The name of the town is derived from the word Loni, or, in Sanskrit, Lavana, on account of its being the centre of a salt tract. It appears to be a very ancient place and is said to have been founded by Shahbuddin Ghauri who ejected the Rajputs and put in their places a body of Mughals. Pathans have been the Zamindars of the surrounding lands which once belonged to Prithviraj, King of Delhi, the remains of whose fort are still visible. Up to the time of Shah, the Emperor of Delhi, there was another broken-down fortress of the Hindu period known as the fort of Raja Sab Karan. It was destroyed by Mahmood Shah and the bricks were used for building a tank and a garden. At Uldipur, there is a fine grove known as Zeenat Mahal, named after the wife of Bahadur Shah. It is surrounded by a brick wall and close to it there is a Rest Home with gates. In the grove there is a scarlet-domed Baradari (Twelve Door) Numerous relics of the Mughul period exist. There is another grove at Loni known as Bagh Ranap which was built about 400 years ago. The walls are built of bricks. There are several other historic monuments in the neighbourhood.

Loni is frequented by foreign and Indian tourists who are attracted to this historic and picturesque town belonging to the epic period dating earlier than 1000 B.C..

40

The Geisha Land of Japan

I have been to Japan several times, but I always recollect my first visit to that fascinating country 40 years ago, when I was received by Emperor Hirohito who has been reigning for 45 years. Hirohito means "the exalted". When a Japanese Emperor begins his reign, he is given another name and when he dies he is known by the adopted name. Hirohito's reign is called *"showa"* (radiant piece) and when he dies he will be known as Emperor Showk.

Emperor Hirohito, the 124th Emperor of Japan, whose ancestors have been reigning over the island empire for the last 2500 years, is referred to by his subjects as Taishi Sama, the son of heaven. A Japanese Emperor is never crowned. He only ascends the throne. He considers himself to be Divine and prays only to his ancestors.

His Highness Maharaja Jagatjit Singh of Kapurthala and I were presented to the Emperor by Sir John Tilley, the British Ambassador, in the private room of audience at the palace in Tokyo. This room was well-furnished with glittering chandeliers hung from the ceiling, and a huge artistic old Japanese vase with large and beautiful white chrysanthemum. The Emperor was in military uniform and decorations. There was only one chair in the room on which no one sat. Therefore, the conversation took place between the Emperor, the Maharaja and myself with all of us standing. Later in the evening we were invited to a large garden party called Chrysanthemum Festival to celebrate the season in the beautiful gardens at Shinjuku at the Royal Tea House where the Emperor entertains his special and distinguished guests. All the noble Japanese gentlemen and diplomats were in frock suits with top hats, just like in London at the Buckingham Palace, while the ladies were dressed in the National dress — Kimono.

The Imperial Hotel on Tuesday morning resembled an exchange bureau for silk hats. Men were hunting for friends and often strangers who had made the remark a few weeks ago that they had high hats to loan if the occasion demanded. The occasion did demand, and high hats were changing hands, quite ostentatiously in the hotel in preparation for the Imperial garden-party on Tuesday afternoon. Many of the delegates who were privileged to attend the function were, of course, without the necessary headgear, and so it was up to several Japanese as well as foreign residents of Tokyo to provide the much-needed article for the guests.

And what was more trying for the delegates was the fact that they were requested to don frock-coats for the occasion. The ladies were more easily accommodated as to their apparel. The Japanese dress, in office and home alike, is their national Kimono. I observed at this garden-party that the refreshments included a bag of sweets at each table for each guest who was supposed to take back these gifts of sweets from the palace for distribution to their families and so forth. As a matter of fact, these bags of sweets given by the Emperor of Japan were taken by the majority of Japanese as well. Such was the reverence the people had for their Emperor in those days.

There is also a Cherry Blossom Festival in April when cherry trees laden with pink and white blossoms mingle with the crimson of the peach blossom as the petals fall on the ground. To see the cherry trees in bloom is a unique sight about which many Japanese poets have written lovely poems.

The bowing ceremony in Japan was remarkable. When two people met, they went on bowing to each other, the junior bowing lower than the senior, and the bowing continued till the senior stopped bowing in response to the bowing of the junior. No country in the world could surpass Japanese in courtesy and mutual respect.

The wife in Japan was treated as unequal to the husband, and when the husband came back home from the office, the wife had to bow, and in the street she had to walk behind her husband. Complete obedience at home was the law for a Japanese family.

A very interesting feature in the life of the Geisha girls is that they entertain their guests most lavishly, though they are most expensive. An hour with the Geisha girls with rice wine will cost a fortune. When the Geisha girls entertain you with wine and music, the cost is about Rs. 500 in terms of cash and gifts for a couple of hours. The millionaires and holiday-seekers from all over the world visit the Geisha girls. But some of the old Japanese people, after an hour or so, get tired of staying with the Geisha girls and return home, preferring to sleep with their wives. However their wives goad them to go back to these girls so that the money spent on them by their husbands would not be wasted.

At present, the Geisha bar and cabaret hostesses face competition from a new generation of women in their 20s and 30s with modern ideas about marriage.

Television and cinema films are bringing a rapid change in the old ideas of submissiveness of the Japanese wife.

The joint family system in the cities is breaking up, leading to a number of love marriages without the permission of the parents. A wealthy man in Japan formerly had his Nigosan (Honourable No.2) or a Geisha or a cabaret girl. This was considered respectable and was expected of a man of position and status and the bill was sent home to his wife to be processed along with laundry and kitchen bills.

Even today, keeping a mistress is commonplace among wealthy men of the older generation, but now the husband who indulges in such luxury must do so on the quiet, in accordance with the changing social values and proprieties. However, the social climate is more in favour of Japanese husbands than the husbands in any other country. Wealthy businessmen and politicians choose to visit old Geisha houses in Akasaka or the glittering cabarets of the Ginza where nude girls bedecked with diamonds act as hostesses to please their clients and guests.

In Tokyo, there are dozens of small-scale Ginzas with a grand total of over 35,000 bars managed by more than 4,00,000 bar girls. The bar girls in Japan play the same role in sociological terms that the Geisha girls play. The Japanese bar is generally a small cosy select place where the girls get to know their customers better.

Sixty per cent of the men are engaged in extra-marital sexual activity in Japan. Thus emerges a new compromise process between arranged marriages and ardent love affairs Divorce is much more of a serious matter for women in Japan than in Western countries. Confucian Ethics make the mother in Japan literally indispensable. Once the mother gets children she is not much of a wife for the husband. The Japanese place absolute value on the serenity and peace of home.

In spite of the movement for the emancipation of women, Japan remains the ideal country where the relations between the husband and the wife are most cordial with harmony and happiness prevailing at home.

41

Focus on Sweden

In Sweden, illegitimate children or their descendants inherit from their mother and her relatives, and the relatives are entitled to inherit from such illegitimate children as if they were born in wedlock. Illegitimate children and their father inherit from each other only under certain circumstances. There exists no right of inheritance between the illegitimate child and the father's relatives.

Adopted children and their descendants inherit as if they were the adopter's children in wedlock. Adoption cuts off the right of inheritance between the adopted child and the natural relatives, except that if one spouse adopts the child of the other spouse, then the right of inheritance is the same as if the child were the mutual child of the spouses. If no heirs are found, the estate goes to a so-called inheritance fund to promote the education and upbringing of children.

A statement of the assets and liabilities of the deceased must be drawn up and signed within three months after the death and registered with the appropriate court within one month. No distribution of an estate can take place until the debts of the deceased are paid. In case an heir is unwilling to accept the debts, he must put the estate in bankruptcy or call for the appointment of a special Administrator within one month after the date of inventory of assets and liabilities is filed.

Certain international circumstances with regard to the assets are provided for by an Act of March 5, 1937.

DIVORCE

(MARRIAGE ACT OF JUNE 11, 1920)

Where married people find it impossible to continue to live together on account of deep and permanent disagreement, they may apply to court, jointly or separately, for a decree of separation. Such a decree, as a rule, will be granted when applied for by either spouse under the following circumstances:

(1)   Where one party has definitely neglected her or his duties to the other or to the children of the union;

(2)   In case of misuse of alcohol or narcotics;

(3)   In case of viciousness, etc. When the parties have lived apart for one year after the separation decree has been granted and have not during that time decided to live together again, divorce is granted on application of either party.

Divorce is granted without prior separation decree for the following reasons: (1) when the husband and wife have been separated on account of domestic discord for a period of three years; (2) when one party spontaneously and without reason deserts the other for two years; (3) bigamy; (4) adultery; (5) gross mistreatment; (6) serious misuse of alcohol or narcotics; (7) insanity; (8) when one party subjects the other to venereal disease; and (9) when sentenced to imprisonment for a long period, etc.

If divorce is granted on the ground that one of the paries has seriously infringed the rights of the other, the latter may secure pecuniary damages.

In connection with decrees for separation or divorce, either party to a marriage may be liable to pay reasonable alimony to the other if it is needed and if the latter is not the principal party at fault.

In case of separation or divorce, the court decides whether the wife or the husband shall have charge of the children. The court, as a rule, tries to make the decision in accordance with the wishes of the parents in case they are in agreement. Otherwise, the court must give its decision with regard to the best interests of the children.

Court decision as to alimony payment or charge of the children may be altered in case the circumstances so justify.

SWEDISH MARRIAGE

"The women stand over fire and bear children" is an old Swedish saying. The husband's role is to provide for the family But now the conception that the husband is the bread-winner is no longer accepted in the Scandinavian countries. In 1840, Scandinavian women had to petition the King for leave to bake bread and sell it. For, the Civil Laws barred them from gainful employment or commercial activity. Almost half of the children were born out of wedlock. The Swedish capital was an enormous brothel, and that was in 1845. In African countries, 3 % of the men learned to read while only 5% of the woman have been given some opportunity; in Pakistan, in 1962, 20% women, in India in the year 1961, 40 % men and 13% women, in Indonesia 57% men and 30% women. The Swedish society had for centuries four important values: (1) patriarchal family system, (2) subordinate role of the women in family life and society, (3) ideal of the mother and house-wife,

(4) abstinence from all sexual activity outside marital life and virginity zeal. The Swedish society today is abandoning these four categories of the ideals of human relationship. Now, in the 70s, they are focused on the content of the equalitarian concept of male and female roles in the family as well as in society. There are no illegitimate children in Sweden, as the law of the country accepts all illegitimate children as legitimate and the society does not condemn illegitimate children.

Here is a model of sexual and family life in Sweden, and let us take Sweden as an illustration for most of the other countries of Europe, particularly the Scandinavian countries. This chapter will give full insight into the laws of marriage, divorce, and different forms of association between two free individuals. It also shows how Swedish society, for centuries, had different standards of social life and how within a very short time new ideals of human relationship have cropped up, particularly from the 20s to the 60s of this century. The present Swedish marriage code was enacted around 1915. The structure of marriage and family is now being debated. The isolated nucleus of the traditional family is being criticised. New types of families and their personal relationships are discussed and experimented by modern group families as well as by the one-parent families. There are trial marriages, group marriages, sometimes also involving group sex and communal group living. All these forms have come with the shifting of the social roles of husband and wife and to the changes in the pattern where one of the parents works away during the week.

There is a growing disregard for sex as the basic mode of differentiation. Boys and girls are given equal roles as the demands could be uniform on both the sexes in relation to the duties of citizenship, economic contribution and creativity.

Divorce denotes 13% in Sweden, U.S.A. 2.5%, U.K. 0.9%

France 0.7%, West Germany 1%. Even if a woman is at fault and connected with adultery, children from the wedlock remain in the custody of the wife and the husband has to give her maintenance for herself and the children.

SWEDISH FAMILY LIFE

Society and values are not static. They change from time to time, conditioned by many other influencing factors. Each period in history has a different set of demands. Society adjusts itself to these requirements though slowly and imperceptibly. Sweden affords an interesting study in this respect in modern Europe.

Before the advent of the present century, like many other European or world societies, Swedish men and women believed in marital fidelity, predominance of man and the inferior status of women.

Democracy, liberty and equality have permeated the family life. Now men and women enter into a voluntary and free union in marriage with the recognition of their responsibility, mutually to the marriage and individually to each other, in full consciousness of the needs and desires of each other.

Old customs deprive a woman of all her privilege, and rights after marriage and subordinates her to the authority of the man. This practice is a corollary of the ancient belief that in patriarchal society, the man is the supreme authority. Diarchy was ruled out and the monarchial concept was applied to the family life as well.

The industrial revolution, modern economy, working women, emancipation of women and the concept of equality have changed the mode of thinking and the pattern of behaviour in Sweden. Such experiments as group living, week-end living, experimental loving and easy divorce have thrown new methods to be experimented by the modern youth. The sum-total of all these trends is a new society with changed social values and new morality in Sweden.

A public debate has been on about the desirability and utility of marriage. The participants in this debate are both men and women, teachers and nuns, the married and the divorced. New ideas are emerging from this debate. Marriage is not an indispensable requirement either for happiness, security or the care of children. One can stay unmarried, give birth to a child, bring up the child with excellent care and yet continue to live with the man from whom the child is born. Legalising of marriage is considered superfluous by some because the desire to have such a legality is created only by the need for social approval. When society ceases to look at such a way of life as immoral or undesirable, the natural consequence is to ignore the formal processes that do not have any value any more.

This new climate solves the problem of the old people and the lonely ones. They get companions more easily and without the painful attendant formalities of legislation.

Trial marriages in the forties afforded a chance for young persons to try for emotional adjustments. Now premarital sex life is accepted as normal and there is no stigma on it which makes matters smooth for living in free love.

The moral concepts regarding child-bearing too have undergone fundamental changes. Child-bearing is not the only function of a woman. Reproduction is not the fundamental requirement of marriage. In this over-populated world, with merciless competition, scarcity of resources and limited employment potential, it is no longer a sacred duty to give birth to a child. A woman may choose to remain childless or to have one child if she so desires. Society looks upon this approach as sensible and even more acceptable.

Margaret Mead has well summarised these trends and says that by 2000 A.D. the present family style of living may be effective in creating a new pattern with emphasis on small families. Thus people would be free to function for the first time in history as individuals. All children will grow in a free atmosphere, with emotional stability, educational facility and economic security, irrespective of the circumstances under which they are born. There will be legal equality and rights for all children irrespective of the nature of the wedlock.

The ethical approach to the problem had involved the Church also in the public debate. Some doubts were raised as to the base of the church getting undermined if the new concepts are accepted. But the vast majority swung the balance in favour of the new concepts and new ways of life. There is no serious objection from the Church due to radical thought pervading the whole of society. The State views the problem more practically. Boys and girls are given equal opportunities in every sphere of activity. There are no separate groups of professions exclusively for girls or for boys. Even knitting and tool handling are no exceptions. Integrated sex education is given in common classes for boys and girls.

The Government of Sweden wants to extend the right of equality in all areas of life to men and women. It appointed a Commission for improving the laws so as to guarantee this concept of equality. This state and society are moving cooperatively together to accomplish this task of putting new trends on a secure and sensible basis.

Sexual and family life ethics in a country are never anything static or independent but are more or less a part of the existing cultural and value system. It has its personal sides and values its privacy — but it is also linked with different parts of the entire structure of the society, such as the economic system, the labour market, the educational system, social welfare and the sex roles system.

FROM TWENTIES TO SIXTIES

Sweden was shifting over from the old traditional patriarchal views of family life with its subordinate role of women towards a new family life, basically founded on democratic marriage and divorce laws. Couples are now able to realise the ideal of "an association between two free individuals, with a mutual obligation to respect each other's needs and wishes" and they have equal responsibility and rights of guardianship for the children. In case of separation or divorce, the possibility exists for voluntary agreement between husband and wife without either partner being branded as the guilty one.

The new family laws, striving for basic equality between the sexes, are fervently progressing in Sweden.

"In the field of private law, an unmarried woman enjoys generally the same rights as man. Marriage, however, has in a great number of countries the effect of depriving the woman of a number of important rights, personal rights as well as property rights. This is due to the fact that traditionally and for centuries the husband has been considered as the head of the family vested with the exercise of marital and parental authority over the person and over the property of his wife and his children."

New types of families, in most cases, should be regarded as serious attempts at creating better emotional conditions for the children and adults alike.

It is not only the angry young men and women who question the happiness of the traditional family system; it is keenly questioned both in the intellectual public debate going on and in practical life. At the annual meeting for Home Economics teachers in the summer of 1969, Monica Beethius, one of Radio Sweden's leading women, was invited to speak. She summarised three points as to why there need be alternative to the traditional family in the new society:

1.   The single individual is a reality in the new society.

2.   The contraceptive technique is safe and will be absolutely safe in future.

3.   Women's emancipation is a reality.

Even within the Christian groups, the traditional style of family life is being questioned. In the spring of 1969, Sweden's first ordained woman minister in the Lutheran Church, Margit Sahlin, invited to a conference of religious and political leaders to discuss this question, said: "Are we mature enough for a new way of living?" with such provocative subtitles as "Are we the last married generation?" and "Stay single — a creative possibility?" Among the speakers and panel members were a Catholic nun, a Lutheran minister, a marriage counsellor and radical leaders from social spheres and practical life and spokesmen of the new family styles. One concrete example of the new types of relationships is Birgitta Dah, Member of Parliament, divorced and pregnant by the man with whom she lives. She stated in a newspaper interview that she does not plan to marry as she believes that the traditional family has ceased to be meaningful. The couple feel free to give the child the best care in an unmarried relationship. With the fast-growing and more open acceptance of various types of companionship without legal marriage, more and more possibilities are resolving the recognised emotional and sexual needs of the individual, male and female alike. Here is a telling example.

A 22-year-old woman journalist said, "Freedom of choice

is so important for the modern woman. But I suppose this is more difficult for a man to accept. I love the man I am with now. We have both a good sexual relationship and a good stable emotional relationship. But I do not feel mature enough to marry and have children yet."

For older people as well, there is a greater acceptance of living together without being married. A widow and a bachelor might find that they have much warmth and feeling to give each other, both emotionally and sexually. But they feel too old to start a family. They live in different communities and both have their professional life, she as a teacher and he as a businessman. They meet during week-ends, are invited together to friends, travel on vacation together, and so on. Thus the possibility of recognizing their needs of independence and companionship has enriched their private lives as well as given them more impetus for their professional work.

Old people are often very lonely, but now they have greater possibilities of finding mutual closeness without taking the big step of marriage. Even in the publicity for homes for the elderly, the question of improving the facilities for the couple to enjoy a relationship, married or otherwise, is under discussion.

Many couples may be much bothered about the solution of married crisis, that is, either to stay together in the traditional way, or to separate or divorce. In the future society, there will be other ways to handle a crisis in a relationship, as already we have new anti-traditional and more flexible possibilities.

OTHER NEW TRENDS

Another noticeable trend is towards trial marriages for deciding if the couple could have a good sex life together. This is often a way of making the relationship acceptable to the family and the community. Now when pre-marital sex is admitted in most circles, there is a new type of "trial marriage" for experiencing if the couple can cooperate in every way, living together, and if their relationship emotionally has a solid enough ground for a family with children.

Another group are the young people who settle down together without reflecting too much. If they find they get along well, both emotionally and sexually, they decide to get engaged and marry, or decide to live in a "loyalty marriage."

The psychological consequences of the general revaluation of roles for men and women may be observed in some of the advanced young couples. Some of them stay voluntarily childless, feeling that it is unethical to give birth to more children in this overpopulated world while others have one or two children of their own and then adopt children from deprived areas in other countries, which is their way of taking responsibility in the global context. Consequently, the value of womanhood is not tied down to child-bearing as in olden times and the value of manhood is not confined to biological reproduction.

This trend may be perceived in the direction which Margaret Mead visualises for the pattern of relations between men and women towards the year 2000. She says:

There would be a growing disregard for sex as a basic mode of differentiation. Boys and girls would be given similar education and like demands would be made on them for citizenship, economic contribution and creativity.

WHAT ABOUT CHILDREN?

Perhaps children will have better possibilities of growing up and maturing if the society becomes more tolerant towards children's various backgrounds and accepts that every child born should have the same legal status and the same chances of educational and emotional security. This involves the society's accepting the child's integrity.

In Sweden, there exists a rather solid base for giving all children the same status and possibilities in life, thanks to the acceptance of the child born out of wedlock on equal terms as the child born inside wedlock and of divorce as a possibility between consenting adults. Thus one does not find in Sweden many children of deserted families as in other societies which reject any relationship other than that of traditional indissoluble family.

This is the new concept of one-parent families, in reality, legally, emotionally and practically. And in family life, education in schools, discussing different types of family relations, the one-parent families comprise a group including not only those headed by unmarried mothers but even those headed by divorcees, widows, widowers and the unmarried.

From the Church's point of view, it is a dilemma as to how much and how far the religious aspects of marriage and sex life should adjust to the society and the broader spectrum of possibilities of various types of stable relationships.

As an example, a group of prominent Christians, including a woman Doctor of Medicine, have tried to align the Church more closely with human reality, in a new report on Love and Marriage. The report says in summary:

"The Church maintains that life-long marriage is the ideal marriage. But knowing that separation and divorce are a reality, the Church's moral code condemning divorce would in fact be succouring a double morality."

And further:

"Sexual relations between two persons who feel closeness

towards each other should be tolerated by the Church while encouraging them to marry."

This new ethical approach has caused many debates and controversies inside the Church. Some groups think that this is to break up the basic Christian ethics for human inter-personal relationship and demand that persons making this type of suggestions resign from their positions inside the Church or retract their statements.

Just as on the international religious scene, the ethical questions are constantly and vividly being debated in Sweden.

WHAT ABOUT SOCIETY?

The new tasks of men and women in society and at home do not only mean changing roles for women but also the emancipation of men that involves retraining men to take their own share of the household chores and of child care. Experience shows that women are often subjected to double work if this retraining of men is not a reality.

The Government's aim that men and women should have the same possibilities in the labour market and in political life, as well as in family life, is reflected even in the new comprehensive schools system of 1962. The traditional subjects for girls are now for boys and girls alike. They have common subjects of study, including child care. Boys are learning sewing and knitting just as girls are learning to use tools and do machine work. Needless to say, both boys and girls have the integrated sex education programme together.

Again, it may be added that, in principle, all Swedish political parties agree that there should be equality between the sexes in all areas of life in the future society. As the former Prime Minister of Sweden said, "The achievement of equality between the sexes not only implies that women will catch up with men in professional life and exercise the same social influence, but also implies that men will have more occasions to observe the child and to exercise their influence on the education of the new generation." Thus the problems of women also become the problems of men.

The latest active step taken by the Government in the summer of 1969 was to appoint a new Commission in order to revise and improve the marriage and family laws in accordance with the new strings for equalisation between men and women. Privileges should not be given to any specific marriage and family type. It is expected that the Commission needs three years of work to find the necessary ways and means of regulating the practical areas.

42

Sex Parks in European Capitals

EUROPEAN CAPITALS

Continuing the account of social and sex life in European countries, I wish to give an account of sexual indulgence in some of the capitals of Europe.

In Copenhagen, in the park called Trivoli, sexual intercourse between men and women are seen freely and openly in most of the nooks and corners of the park, regardless of the fact that onlookers are there to watch their performance. Those who are in action are not at all worried about the onlookers who stand and watch them. Not only do men and women come there by previous appointment to indulge in sex, but those men who are erotically adventurous go there and find girls of their choice.

Then there is a grassy plot at the far end of Bois de Boulogne near Paris where similar acts take place on the ground and it is unabashedly called in colloquial French "parterre". One sees dozens of cars landing up there in the evening and the occupants leaving their cars and lying down on the grass for indulging in sex.

In Honolulu, at the Waikiki beach, one sees hundreds of couples lying on top of each other with scanty clothing, sometimes nude, basking in the sun without any interference from the police. Though they are not seen indulging in the sex act, the semblance gives an indication from a distance that these couples are performing the act of love. Similar is the case in the Vaves. Merry-making boys and girls go out in rowing boats and remain under the trees for hours together, unmindful of whether the passers-by are watching them or not.

Hyde Park in London has always been the magnet for the sex-hungry. Hundreds of couples openly indulge in the sex act with no screen or cover around them except for an umbrella put on one side.

In many of the main capitals of Europe, the system of having a mistress along with one's wife is not uncommon. I attended many official lunches and dinners where the Ministers of the Governments of European countries were present, and at the time of the toast, I found that the Ministers were drinking to the health and happiness of their mistresses rather than their wives at the same table. I was sitting next to a Frenchman. I asked him whom this particular Minister was toasting. He whispered in my ear that she was his mistress. I may also mention here that the wives are not ignorant of the fact that the husbands are getting their mistresses invited to the same functions where they are invited. As the mistresses generally belong to a high state of society and most of them are celebrated personalities, nobody raises a finger at them although the society people know who is involved with whom.

I asked a friend from Sweden about the free marriages and free love being practised. He gave me a long explanation for more than an hour. He said that in European countries, particularly in the Scandinavian countries, people have reached a high degree of civilisation and culture and they feel they should be more natural by adopting the same system of free love as their primitive ancestors had adopted, with one difference — that the primitives did not know what they were doing while the educated men, with all the knowledge and education behind them, are in a better position to understand and appreciate the affinity with Nature which the modern individuals feel inspired to attain. This explains the origin of the movement of free love in most parts of Europe and America. It is only in those countries where the Church is still strong that people have a horror of misusing man-made laws and the control of man over woman is strong and fewer people are indulging in free love.

When I am talking about the morals or the way of life in some of the European countries, I have in mind only the elite of the society, the aristocracy and the higher middle class. It is only this stratum of society which frames laws and sets the pace of cultural evolution in the country, to be emulated by the lower middle class and the lowest stratum of society. In all countries of the world which I visited, I found infidelity and immorality more in practice among the upper classes than in the lower ones and the same is the case in India.

43

The Netherlands Scene

In Amsterdam in the Netherlands, and Copenhagen in Denmark, theatres and cinema halls have live shows. Group marriages are common. It is common for married couples to advertise in the newspapers, soliciting the company of other married couples interested in exchanging wives, and such advertisements are readily responded to. A red light behind fashionable restaurants indicates that there are girls available for sexual satisfaction. They sit at tables which are for two persons. The visitor can sit at any of the vacant tables and join the girl of his choice.

The remarkably unbelievable phenomenon is that newspapers publish pornographic material which in any other country would be banned.

There was a film fair in Copenhagen where sex poses were shown to the public in a way similar to any other feature film, and it was an international film fair and attracted tourists from all over the world.

Then, for attracting tourists, there was a festival called "wet-dream" where all kinds of sex poses were shown at the theatre.

Naturally, it attracted large crowds of tourists. The festival and the film fair were organised by the Government and created a sensation all over the world.

In California, today one talks of sexual liberation since the first of July 1970 when a law was passed authorising abortion in New York State. More than a hundred thousand abortions have taken place since then in New York alone and in the State of Washington, Alaska and Hawaii where abortion is legal. Women from foreign countries come to reside there for a while and take shelter of the law for abortion to get rid of unborn children. Statistics show that half of the abortions in these States are solicited by married women.

Besides, many hospitals perform the operation for abortion. There are private institutions called Women's Lib which advertise for such operations in the Press for the 'benefit' of University students.

At Miami beach during the Christmas holidays, one aeroplane flew regularly low above the place advertising the name, telephone number and address of the firm for information on abortions.

If you spend week-ends at Topenga Canyon in California, you will be amazed to find a sexual therapy centre at a distance of 10 miles from Los Angeles between the sea and the holiness associated with a place like Santa Monica. Here there are groups of psychiatrists, psycholoques and masseurs to give you physical harmony if you are losing sexual power or if you are suffering from nervous breakdown.

To get the therapeutic treatment called 'Seance de Toucher', each man has to pay 100 dollars. There inside you are surrounded by several beautiful girls — all naked. To sit and act in a group is called 'sexuality of the group' or 'marathon of the naked'.

Most of the men who get the treatment come out satisfied, their failing vigour restored. The head of the institution is a pastmaster in the therapeutic treatment and the whole process is regulated like in a private hospital.

I went to Europe recently and saw with my own eyes the various changes that have taken place in the social life of the Europeans. Though I have been visiting Europe very often and probably have been there over 40 times, I have been noticing gradual changes in the social life of the people in all walks of life since my visit to Europe over 50 years ago and my subsequent visits in the last decade. Therefore, what I write now is from my personal experience and not from hearsay.

In the Metro in Paris, one finds young men and women embracing each other before the public and they are not at all shy of clasping each other closely and hugging and kissing. This is considered to be a part of the social life of the country and the present mood of the youth of France. I made inquiries from my French friends as to why this was allowed. They replied that there was nothing immoral in kissing and hugging. Again, I was surprised to see dozens of couples lying in the lawns of Cite Universitaire in Paris — young students, boys and girls of mature age lying on the grass, hugging and kissing. I asked the student, whose guest I was for lunch that afternoon at the Cite Universitaire, to take me to a Professor of the University. He arranged for me to talk with two Professors of the University. They told me "We do not stop young boys and girls who are sexually inclined to participate in this particular form of enjoyment". However, one of them said, "We will not allow them to have a proper sexual intercourse on the lawns." He explained fully to me that out of 100 students between the ages of 18 and 26, at least 20 to 30 per cent are maniacs. The rest of the students are inclined to be free from uncontrollable sex impulses and occupy their time in pursuit of knowledge. A good percentage of them are there only for art, philosophy or painting, and the rest are completely immune to the attraction of women. He further told me that if they disallow this 20 to 30 per cent of the girls and boys who like to indulge in kissing and hugging and lying close to each other, they will be going out of the University campus to indulge in sex.

And similar is the case in the social life of France. The French are more inclined to have a home life than some of the other nations in Europe, though France is known to be the home of gaiety and frivolity and adventures in sex matters. Monsieur Andre de Fouquieres, a personal friend of mine who was a leader of the Parisian society at that time, told me that in Paris there were two channels of life, one is family life or home life, and the other is gutter life where people can indulge in sexual affairs abundantly. He said, "We don't mix up the two". They are like two rivers flowing side by side but not merging into each other and this was also the view of many distinguished Frenchmen. While in the Scandinavian countries there is free love, it is not the case in France at present though France is also rapidly changing and coming into the orbit of the new ways of the Scandinavian society. A Frenchman told me that adultery is considered to be committed only if it happens inside the residential house of the married couple. For instance, if a Frenchwoman has illicit sexual connection with any man outside the house, the husband is not inclined to divorce her and vice versa is the case with the husband.

If there is any disturbance in the French society for moral degradation, it is due to the law passed in 1946.

Sexual indulgence in French society is aggravated by the closing of the houses of prostitution in 1946. The new Brothel Bill was sponsored by a De Gaullist Deputy in the National

Assembly of France. In addition, he had the blessing of the woman who was responsible for closing the houses of prostitution in 1948, Madame Martha Richard.

The 1946 law closed even the pleasure places like the House of Nations and the Sphinx, but it did not outlaw prostitution as such. It simply made it illegal to operate a house of prostitution or to solicit for the purpose of prostitution.

Prostitution is in the form of Call Girl Services, Casual Pick-up in the Metros and the Bars, and discreet as well as blatant street soliciting. There is hardly any hotel in Paris which would interfere with a man entertaining a lady in his room.

Recently, I came to know that some nudist clubs which were in the past known for their exclusiveness, and stayed away from the public eye, have now declared that they would no longer keep nudity a secret. Now there are nudity clubs in such areas and places where they are seen by the public at large. According to them, to be nude is not a crime nor is it against any social order. It is also reported in some newspapers that the Queen of England congratulated them on their taking this bold step and for their cult of nudity which, being in accordance with the view of the Queen, gives vigour and strength to the participants in the nudity club.

Again, in the U.S.A., in some of the churches the clergy preaches to congregations composed largely of nude persons. It is also reported that the clergymen congratulated the persons for remaining nude, thus following the law of nature. So if clergymen and the Heads of States encourage nudity, this cult will spread all over the world and nudity would be accepted and put within the framework of the laws of more and more countries.

Recently, in New Delhi, a Dutch citizen by the name of

Jacque de Mani was found naked and sentenced to 10 days' imprisonment. After 10 days, he was released and again he started walking about in Connaught Place absolutely naked. When re-arrested, he started shouting, "I have come to this world naked and no man can stop me from walking naked." He was again sentenced to 20 days' imprisonment. But then he found life in the prison hard, and as he could not go naked there, he committed suicide by tying a handkerchief around his neck. I spoke to many Americans and Europeans about this episode. They told me that it was unjust for the Judge to sentence him to imprisonment. The most he ought to have done was to warn him and to put him in a psychiatric institution for treatment, but sentencing him to imprisonment was against all ethics and the natural inclination of man. Such are the feelings and views of the ordinary man in Europe and America. From the above narration alone, one can sense in what direction the wind is blowing and in which way society in the West is moving.

44

France of Today

It is interesting to describe here what sort of life women lead in France today, by giving an account of the French society which is much less sexually emancipated than the those of Scandinavian countries and the U.S.A.. In France, which is predominantly a Catholic country, there are still restrictions on the morals of boys and girls, but the influence of other European countries is slowly removing them. In their private life, French people do not have the same freedom for youthful exuberance as in other countries. The French have always been inclined to live in their family circle, but the family influence in the Grande Bourgeoisie and the Bonne Bourgeoisie is diminishing. General de Gaulle, the great President of France, belonged to the Grande Society while Monsieur Michel Debre, the present Defence Minister of the Government of France, belongs to the Bonne Bourgeoisie.

Arranged marriages have almost disappeared in France and this has brought about great personal freedom. Grown-up children of responsible families of France can revolt against the traditions of their families without being considered undesirable. The social difference between the aristocracy and lower middle class in France is disappearing with such speed that there is a possibility that the distinctions may disappear in a short time.

Some of the Chateaus that I visited have been sold by the aristocracy to the rich families and the industrialists.

In France, the average families live together. As defined in the Code Napoleon of 1804, there is complete unity of thought and affection among the members of the family, though within the last 10 years or so the ties of affection among the members of the families have loosened considerably. Even now foreigners are seldom admitted in the family circle for dinner parties or festivals unless they are very friendly with the members of the family. As I said before, the French are traditionally family-loving people, but that tradition is slowly dying out under the influence of countries like England, Sweden, Holland, America and others. Now the couples hardly spend their Sundays with their parents as they used to do in former times, and instead of remaining at home during holidays, they go out to foreign countries to spend holidays and week-ends in secluded places, like the seaside or holiday resorts. The affinity which existed in most of the families of France, particularly in the higher classes of the Parisian society, no longer exists.

Young people make their own choice for marriage. Arranged marriages have disappeared, except in the old and orthodox families.

As divorce is easily obtainable, the divorce figures in France are at the rate of one in every ten marriages. As France is a secular state, divorce is not a difficult thing to obtain; it is only expensive. It may also be mentioned that there are more divorces in Paris than in the provinces. In 1964, a Bill was passed giving more legal rights to women to divorce as well as to own property. But the majority of women do not believe in feminism; they care more for femininity. French women, even though they are in service or politics, are seductive and sexy. They take care of their figure and complexion unlike the suffragette women of England and the U.S.A. who, when in politics or high office, look more manly and neglect their dresses. Women in France are not debarred from holding any post but they seldom like to contest elections and aspire for high positions. Their number in the National Assembly dropped from 30 in 1945 to 11 in 1967. In the Elections, only 2 per cent of the candidates were women, compared with 26 women M.P.s in England. Women in France are not inclined to enter public life and prefer to wield their influence on their husbands in politics from behind the scene just as it is in the case of Madame Charles de Gaulle and Madame George Pompidou, the consort of the President of France. Besides, women want to create a lovable impression on their husbands and get things done without having legal rights. They very seldom go to court for litigation. In France, before the Matrimonial Bill of 1964 which abrogated the old laws that forbade women from opening bank accounts or obtaining passports, the wife's infidelity was considered more serious than her husband's desertion and infidelity.

As men have contempt for the masculine type of women, feminism is despised by them and this is one of the reasons why Frenchwomen prefer to stay as mistresses of the house and look after the husband and children. It is of course considered an exception when women with scanty economic means have to seek jobs in offices, shops and other places. The majority of such women are married.

In spite of the great struggle going on all over Europe and America, Frenchwomen still hold their own. They have not given up their home-life, though, of course, a great percentage of teenage girls have taken to the new life of free love and amusement. Frenchwomen are romantic and seldom virgin before marriage. It is a false idea of the world tourists who visit France that Frenchwomen are *'le'gere'* and that France is a land of unfettered love and sex. From my personal experience of 40 visits to France, I can say that this is not true. The reason why this idea has gone round the world is that the tourists are unable to distinguish between the domestic life of the French people and the gay and hectic life in Montmartre or the night life and free Jove life on the left bank of Seine. This impression is also due to the fact that the French domestic life is not open to foreigners except for a few personal friends who are permitted to enter the inner circle of the French family. But those like myself who have lived among French families from childhood, and even now are received in the highest aristocratic as well as bourgeois families, know exactly and intimately their way of life.

However, I must confess that I find a great change from the time when I was a student in Paris and lived with a French family to a couple of years ago when I was the guest of a French family. I find a great difference between the material outlook of the women of 1914 and those of 1970. In the early years of the twentieth century, girls in the family had secret love affairs before their marriage with two or more boys, whether French or foreigners, and kept the secret to themselves not revealing it even to their mothers. But now women openly carry on their romances to the knowledge of their mothers and the whole family, and even to the knowledge of their husbands who reconcile themselves by having two or three women as their mistresses. It is not considered in any way objectionable or dishonorable as it was in the early twenties. In the early twenties, the mothers forbade the young girls to go out with young boys alone to cinemas and theatres. It was not permitted at that time by society. But now students and working girls have become very free and teenage girls are anxious to lose their virginity as they wish to imitate the girls of their age in the Scandinavian countries in their amorous adventures. Women who have children out of wedlock are called 'Mama Celibataire' and to be called as such is not considered a crime or dishonour. Only 27 per cent of the girls under 30 approve of premarital sex even between fiancés and 12 per cent of such children in France are conceived before wedlock. As religion and Catholic ideals of chastity are removed from the minds of the girls and parents, religion's hold has completely vanished and there are more pre-marital love affairs than ever in the history of France. In France, love affairs and scandals are not deterrents to girls going out of their way to entangle themselves in sexual love, nor do the French people take any note of such scandals unlike in England where John Profumo, a Minister in the British Cabinet got entangled with a woman of low morals leading to his resignation and creating a national crisis. From my conversations with young women and teenagers in France and other countries of Europe, I had a feeling that they are now unable to bear the strain of keeping their love affairs a secret and they cannot afford to spend their nights without their lovers. This strain has given them mental suffering and they want to break the chains of social rules of behaviour and character.

Then there is a big difference between the behaviour of Englishwomen and that of Frenchwomen. If you take any Englishwoman to dinner and if after dinner she invites you to her flat or home, it is understood that she is willing to flirt with you. While in France, if you take a girl out and on return she asks you to have a cup of coffee or a drink in her room, it means nothing unless both are agreeable to have courtship or flirtation. There are about one million abortions every year in France, more than the number of live births, in spite of the fact that women use all kinds of uterine washing and periodic abstinence and contraceptives. There is over-indulgence in sex in France and European countries. They go to holiday resorts during the holidays. They don't care for promiscuity but they prefer to indulge in sports and lead a primitive life among men. Many new villages built of straw have been created in Sicily and other islands around it and also in many other nooks of Europe. These villages have been carefully built to satisfy the taste and sophisticated desires of the Europeans and Americans for returning to nature as primitives. There are several seaside places where men and women walk about nude in the streets and remain naked in their homes.

There are two such seaside places which are the paradise of nudists. The place des Domdelene is well frequented where everyone is naked, basking in the sun, swimming, or promenading in the streets without any complex. The other is the De Levant which is half occupied by a military garrison and half by the nudist colony. Even the shopkeepers in the streets are in the nude. As a matter of fact, wearing of clothes is taboo. The climate of these islands is temperate. One does not suffer from cold even if one does not wear clothes.

Some of the restaurants and night clubs in France cater only to the youth. One of these is La Locomotive which is banned to all above 25 years of age. From my personal talks with old and young women of France, I understand that if the school system is changed and the youth are allowed to breathe freely, these strange ideas causing havoc among teenagers will disappear although it is already in the temper of the youth to ignore the advice of their parents.

The hold of religion in the European countries as well as in India and other countries has been diminishing gradually during the last century, and a large number of people have faith in it only outwardly; in their hearts they do not believe in religion as they used to do 50 years ago. Only 14 per cent of the French are Catholic. Religion is still playing some part in rural areas and in the provinces. In churches, the clergy do not preach religion and sermons with the same enthusiasm as they used to have because they know that such sermons have no effect on the people.

Since Communism took root in Russia, the writings of great writers and leaders like Lenin and Marx and celebrated poets have brought a change in the minds of people. Sartre's philosophic books *L'Etre* and *Le Neant* made a great stir in France and Europe. The Existentialist Movement was generated during World War II. Secularism started in some of the countries, and the people became less disposed towards religion and more towards materialism with the result that great qualities of culture and traditional values began to be ignored. People were for gaining material advancement and more and more, they lost faith in religion and even accepted Atheism as their creed.

45

Islands of Love and Laughter

All along the Riviera, there are villages on the Mediterranean coast which have been built by a commercial organisation to meet the French taste for sophistication and individualism amid primitive surroundings. French society gets away from the tension and hustle and bustle of towns and cities to these villages as to islands of fraternity. In these Mediterranean villages, one stays in little Tahitian thatched huts. The visitors put on the brightly coloured Tahitian sarongs. In some villages, the visitors wear flower garlands, beads and necklaces. Drinks, cigarettes and meals in open-air patios are in abundance. Wine is unlimited and is included in the bills. There are open-air dances and sports, concerts and theatres.

ST. TROPEZ — THE NUDIST HEAVEN

St. Tropez, once a modest fishing port, has been turned into a gorgeous recreation and health resort. This place is the rage of the tourists from all over America and Europe. Crowds around the bars and beaches of St. Tropez are immense. Everyone is in a gay and carefree mood.

St. Tropez is situated between Cannes, St. Maxime, Cavalaire, Le Lavandeu, Hyeres and Toulon on the Mediterranean coast and is frequented in the season stating from May, by celebrated cinema stars, beautiful women artists and famous dancers who appear in the most exquisite transparent dresses and swimming costumes and stroll along the streets in minis, midies, maxis and hotpants. Every year women wear less and less clothes on their body. In restaurants and on the beaches, women with beautiful figures are seen with their breasts uncovered. Tourists are amazed to see the women in such nudity on the first and second day of their arrival. But then they get so used to this new fashion that they are rather shocked to see them with their breasts covered. They dance, dine and walk without brassieres. In a small restaurant with rustic wooden furniture, many men and women are huddled together almost fully naked. They are so close to each other in a small restaurant that the bodies of friends and strangers touch each other, creating an erotic stir. Recently, at St. Tropez, Mick Jagger married Vianca Berz Morns de Macias. The religious ceremony took place at the Catholic Chapel of St. Anne and all the members of the Rolling Stone group were present as well as Beatles Paul McCartney and Ringo Star who came from London by a specially chartered plane.

The visitor finds all sorts of sports in St. Tropez — horses to ride, tennis, volleyball, judo, sailing boats, hundreds of skis nautiques, surfboard-riding on the waves, bridge, chess, ping pong, besides gambling and games like Boule along with orchestras, Les Discotheques and late night clubs. There is a lovely beach with white crystal-like sand with bars and restaurants all around to regale the visitors while they are dancing barefoot under the stars and the open sky.

Nature and men have continued to make this lovely place a heaven of pleasure and the joy of living.

This Mediterranean club has three styles of housing accommodation: (i) Le Bungalow En Dur with two beds with complete sanitary installation, hot and cold douche toilet and WC, (ii) Lacase-a polythene case with bamboos on the roofs and two beds with douche (Lababos) and WC and (iii) Le Bungalow de Toile, the modern canvas tent with two or three beds.

Another characteristic of these clubs and villages is that the Manager of the Establishment provides you with tables for lunch and dinner with a few other partners and goes on changing the partner.

What is remarkable at St. Tropez is that it is a small place where so many enthusiasts and lovers of this man-made Mediterranean port collect and enjoy themselves to their heart's content. Bardot, the famous film actress who was inspired to create this gay paradise and was the moving spirit in building it up, built a villa for herself nearby where she spends a few months every year. But as she is mobbed by the crowds and by her adoring friends, she had to put up high walls around her villa. This place is now considered to be the abode of young people who want to be cured of their loneliness by its magic. The place is full of young German, Swedish and American girls and boys. They mix with one other without any formality or restraint.

Girls of about 16 years of age arrive from Paris without money and see how far their personal charm will carry them. In the summer nights, one sees them by the dozens, gaily dressed with fantastic hairstyles and jeans of different colours with scanty clothes on the upper portions of their bodies. One sees them hanging around the bars, particularly at the famous Bar Lescale, waiting for some young enthusiasts to pick them up and pay the bills of their further hotel stay. The girls are ready to make love before marriage as they consider that it is not immoral to live with a man without being married. At the same time, they feel that they are serious girls and their standard of morality is high.

In France women walk about in the streets with dogs. One out of three women in the streets of Versailles, Saint Cloud and Strassburg, which I visited recently, has a pet dog. My son Rakesh, who is studying in Strassburg, told me that women did not wish to go through the hardship of pregnancy, childbirth and looking after the children till they grow up. He told me that they preferred to breed dogs and get attached to them as if they were their children. The angle of thought changes from one period to another. To give birth to a child was of the greatest joy to a mother. Issueless women were condemned by society and even by religion. The Hindu religion preaches that a woman who begets a son not only perpetuates the name of her husband's family, but the son also performs the last rites on the death of his father for the salvation of his soul. Now women in Europe, America and also in most parts of Asia including India, prefer not to have children. Not only do they use all sorts of contraceptives for stopping childbirth, but if perchance they become pregnant, they go for abortion. And since they must have someone to love, they have started to love pet dogs.

Then there are beaches and pleasure resorts which are usually interesting and pleasing. One leaves Gare de Lyons by an Italian train which is bound for Cefalu in Sicily, one of the largest summer villages. Special trains are run in which arrangements are made for dancing and drinking. There is singing and merry-making in the train. In these trains mostly there are young couples who are in love with each other, and they give exuberant expression to their feelings before the other passengers without any inhibition. When the train halts at Cefalu, one is met by lovely hostesses who help one with one's suit-cases, and many men and women dressed in fancy dresses blow all sorts of trumpets and fanfares to greet the passengers. The reception of the visitors is so splendid, genuine and affectionate that they think themselves well-compensated for coming to this glorious place. Small, scantily-furnished huts are allotted to the tourists which are unsophisticated though quite comfortable. Lunch is served in delightful parties with coloured parasols, and the meal is always delicious and palatable. In these seaside places, boys and girls, even older men and women, let themselves go and live with nature and do such things as their hearts dictate without any of the conventions or rules and regulations that govern society. Bathrooms are common and men and women do their toilets together. Meals are served in the common room and there is no restriction regarding the dress. Most of the visitors who partake of these meals are in transparent swimming suits.

46

Church and Morals on the Run

Since 1904, France has been secular and the Church dis-established till recently when the upper Bourgeoisie raised their head to re-establish it. De-Christianisation of France has been going on gradually as in many Western countries for over a century. Most of the French people pay lip-service to Christianity and neglect it entirely except on ceremonial occasions such as marriages and funerals. The traditional respect for priests has declined both as moral and social leaders. The Pope and other Church leaders are fully aware of this phenomenon and are trying hard to bring back faith in Christianity among the French people, as they are afraid that the Communist influence against the Church may turn believers into Atheists.

In the middle of 1960, the Church started an active campaign to re-assert its authority, and this is the reason why the neo-Catholic movement is spreading in France and people are beginning to realise the value of Christianity and the proper meaning of life.

In the old days, the French were well known for "amour" or love-making, while the English had pubs and loved sports.

But now all nations copy one other and there is no special habit or mannerism for any particular nation. Many of the American features of enjoyment are found on the sea-coasts of France, such as barbecues and drug stores, and in such seaside places, it is very difficult to recognise to which nationality an individual belongs.

With every passing year, the mode and morals of Europeans and Americans rapidly change and this year when I went to Europe to see what further changes had taken place in the mentality of people of the European nations, I found to my horror that the sense of morality had gone to the lowest pitch of degradation.

I went to see a much-advertised film called 'Le Souffle au Coeur' by Louis Malle who in an exclusive interview told the reporter: "Of all my films which I have produced, Le Souffle au Coeur is the film which is closest to my heart." This film was being shown in the best cinema halls in Paris and elsewhere in France other as well as European countries. I had to wait for an hour to get a ticket to see this film as there was a long queue.

The story of this film was based on the incestuous sexual perversion of a young boy by the name of Laurant with his mother Clara, 35 years of age. Actual sexual poses and scenes between the son and mother were shown in this film in the Concorde Cinema hall situated in the world famous Avenue des Champs Elysee in Paris. The hall was full of spectators and they seemed to be thrilled with this degrading and immoral film. One can imagine the effect of such a film on the youth of the country when such sexual and incestuous scenes are depicted on the screen between mother and son in an unabashed and vulgar manner. Louis Malle is known to have the reputation of depicting the worst and the hideous side of life as he did in the film which he called 'Calcutta' in which he depicted the miseries of humanity, poverty in the slums of Calcutta. This film was banned in India. The B.B.C. came in for adverse criticism when it screened the film and refused to discontinue the series. The Government of India ultimately asked the B.B.C. to wind up its office in India. The puzzling point is that the producer of such a notorious French film which has been condemned has not been prosecuted, nor has his film been censored. As a matter of fact, to my utter amazement, I found during my stay in Cannes this year that 'Le Souffle au Coeur' was selected for the Cannes film festival. I discussed the merits of this particular film with many highly-placed and distinguished friends, French men and women in Paris, who told me that the film was a notorious one, though they said that some stray cases of sexual relationship between mother and son, brother and sister do occur. But they were very emphatic that these obscene scenes on the screen produce perverse ideas in the minds of the youth and horrify the old.

It must be noted that in France prior censorship of films does not exist. It is only on the premiere of a film that La Vrigade Mondaine sends observers to the film show to verify whether it goes against the morals and good manners of the people, and if the observers find that the film violates Articles 283 and 290 of the criminal code, the Public Prosecutor decides to open a judicial-enquiry against the producers, directors and actors of the film, but so far Le Souffle au Coeur has not been considered as violating the morals and the manners of the people. The producers, directors and others have not been prosecuted as has been the case with a play called 'Oh! Calcutta' played in La Salle des Elysee Montmartre.

Another peculiarity I found during this trip was that men were dressed up, powdered and lipsticked like women with long hair falling on the shoulders. One afternoon, I went to a telegraph office in Paris to send a cable to my wife and asked the clerk attending at the counter in French, "Madame, *voila le cable que je voudrai envoyer.*" This clerk looked at me with surprise and asked me which class of cable I wished to send. From the voice I understood that the person at the counter was not a woman but a man. He did not seem annoyed with me for calling him "Madame" but helped me to send the cable at the cheapest rate, *Tariff de Nuit.*

47

Sex Gap Galore

Here is an interesting account from a newspaper under the heading "Generational Sex Gap".

WASHINGTON-Everyone talks about the problems parents have with their children, but no one is aware that grandparents also have trouble identifying with their grandchildren. A friend of mine whom I shall call Zachary Danbury, decided to take his 16-year-old son to see Zach's mother who was in a nursing home. Mrs. Danbury, in her eighties, was happy to see both of them.

Unfortunately, Zach's son had very long hair and this was when the trouble started.

"Mother," said Zach, "this is my son Bobby."

"She is very beautiful," Mrs. Danbury said.

"No, Mother, Bobby is a boy, not a girl."

Mrs. Danbury nodded. A few minutes later she said, "Bobby, I hope you don't let boys get fresh with you. They lose all respect for a girl if she's considered easy."

Bobby said, "Grandma, I don't go out on dates with boys. I go out on dates with girls."

"That's nice," said Mrs. Danbury. "You will never get into trouble if you go out with girls."

"Mother," said Zach, "you don't understand. Bobby is a boy. That's why he goes out with girls."

Mrs. Danbury absorbed this and then nodded. "I see you wear pants, Bobby. You know when I was a girl we were not permitted to wear pants. When I was your age, my mother made me wear crinolines when I went out. I don't suppose you know what they are."

"No, Grandma, I don't."

Mrs. Danbury smiled, "None of the young girls know what they are any more." Then she peered closely at Bobby and said. "You don't wear lipstick, do you?"

Bobby shook his head. "No, Grandma, I don't.

"You should be very proud of her, Zachary," Mrs. Danbury said to her son, "If you saw some of the young girls who came to visit their grandparents here you'd be appalled," Then she turned to Bobby again. "Can you cook."

"A little," Bobby replied.

"Learn to cook. You will never hold on to a man if you don't know how to cook."

Zachary said, "Mother, Bobby isn't trying to find a man. He is a man, at least he's almost a man."

Mrs. Danbury's eyes gleamed. "Lots of young girls think all they have to do is look sexy. Well, let me tell you something, Bobby. You are beautiful now, but you won't always be beautiful. That's when you need to hold on to your husband. I don't think you are going steady at sixteen?"

"No, Grandma," Bobby said, "I am not going with anybody on a permanent basis."

"That's good," Mrs. Danbury said. "Make all the boys come to you. Never chase them."

"Yes, Grandma."

"I'd like to do something nice for you, Bobby, since you came to see me. Here is $ 20."

"What for?" Bobby asked.

"Buy yourself a pretty dress," Mrs. Danbury said. "I don't have any objection to you wearing pants, but I think you should have one pretty dress in your closet for some special occasion."

Bobby took the $ 20 bill.

"Thank you, Grandma."

"It is all right. Bobby," said Mrs. Danbury and smiled. "Mrs. Dobkins, who lives across the hall from me, is always bragging about her grand-daughter, so I want to see the expression on her face when she sees that I too have a beautiful grand-daughter."

I asked the Frenchman sitting next to me while going to Strassberg whether the feminine looks of men would not lead to homosexuality in greater numbers than before. He replied bluntly "What does it matter? This is the time of life to do what you like. What is wrong with homosexuality? It is only more painful, that is all."

So the whole angle on life is changing for the worse.

ONE YOUNG STUDENT

One young student in Strassberg told me that marriages between sisters and brothers should be encouraged and legalised. I asked him, why? He said this would produce a race of pure genes. I told him that, on the contrary, the race would be reduced to an inferior quality and that is why in most of the countries incest is a crime. He was not convinced. I quoted religious scriptures and moral code from ancient times but he differed from me.

A friend of mine, a Frenchman in Paris, attended a reception given by Mrs. Lindberg who was exhibiting her paintings and had invited three to four hundred members of the high society of Paris including Ministers, Ambassadors and other dignitaries. She appeared in the most fantastic dress, practically nude. Her breasts were covered with ornamental embroidered cloth, but there were apertures on the nipples which were showing. The same was the case with her private parts. Mr. Lindberg was proud of the figure and breasts of his wife.

At another reception, the hostess was nude except for a huge diamond hung to her ring whose platform-like base covered her, while the other feminine guests glittered from head to foot with jewels covering all parts of their bodies and private parts. Every husband felt very proud in introducing his wife to the guests.

Earnest Shakespeare, Associate of the Royal Photographic Society and the Association of the Institute of Incorporated Photographers, sells pornographic film at his studio in Bulwar Road, Leytonstone, London, and is also not averse to amateurs doing it themselves in sex productions on his premises. He hires out models and equipments for the purpose.

To one investigator, he sold a film called Arabian Nights conveying pornographic scenes with the symbol of a snake. He also pays for a group sex association involving more than two pupils. Shakespeare and others in this profession are the hub of the foreign marketers in Denmark, Sweden and Japan where there are associations for pornography. Denmark relaxed its laws in 1964, as big producers need an outlet for sexy projections.

48

Khajuraho the Sanctum of the Sex Arts

Khajuraho, to which most Western tourists make a regular pilgrimage to satisfy their sexual sense, gives them the impression that the Hindu religion is based on sex. They see the erotic statues in Khajuraho temple and other temples in Orissa and South India.

It was in the 12th century that the cult called rammorgies equivalent to the hippie cult started and the worshippers indulged in the sexual poses carved on multifarious stones.

There are various versions about Khajuraho and similar other temples in India. One is that the worshippers, before going to the temple, should see the horrors of sex poses and take a vow for not indulging in them before going to the temple for prayer. The other viewpoint is that the cult of sex orgies was a perversion of Hindu philosophy and culture and the worshippers gave vent to their sex exuberance in many forms and went even to the extent of carving statues and figures in the temples to manifest the perverted doctrine of their cult.

Khajuraho and similar temples in Orissa and other states

depicting sexual poses are a gross insult to Indian culture and civilisation, and the tourists go back to their country with the belief that Indian culture and religion are based only on sex. We should either demolish these temples or forbid foreigners to visit them. For the sake of collecting some foreign exchange from the visits of foreigners to these temples, we should not become the laughing stock of the world. Already, the Hindu religion is misunderstood in Europe and America. The worst impression is created when the foreigners visit such temples. Whatever explanation one may be able to give the visitors about the true interpretation of these sexual poses, they begin to believe that Hindu religion and temples are all dedicated to sex worship.

In Conclusion

So we come to the end of the book.

What imprint does it leave us with?

We perceive that quite early in his life Diwan Jarmani Dass came into contact with wonderful, glamorous and powerful women of the highest strata of Indian as well as European society, and that contact enhanced his entire perception of human society. He not only saw, but observed, the 'society ladies' of changing societies. In the fascinating chapters of this book, he has put together the account of his direct and indirect experiences and contact with them.

He ranges from Sita, Nurjahan and Lakshmibai of India to Ann Boleyn, Josephine and Catherine of Europe, and as we come to the closing lines, we are left with a colorful impression of fascinating women that have forever changed the face of the world they have been born in. They have reigned over the times — and been, in the true sense of the term, Queens or Maharanis.

●●●